TEACHING CHILDREN, EMPATHY, THE SOCIAL EMOTION

Lessons, Activities and Reproducible Worksheets (K-6) That Teach How to "Step Into Other's Shoes"

By Tonia Caselman, Ph.D.

youth light inc.

© 2012, 2010, 2009, 2008, 2007
YouthLight, Inc.
Chapin, SC 29036

Cover Design by Amy Rule
Layout / Graphics by Amy Rule
Project Editing by Susan Bowman

ISBN 1-59850-014-7

Library of Congress Number
2006934786

10 9 8 7 6 5 4
Printed in the United States

ACKNOWLEDGEMENTS

I would like to express my deep appreciation to Rita Adams for her review of the manuscript and to my husband, Steve Jones, who has provided me with huge amounts of encouragement and task support at home. In addition, I would like to thank all of the children who have allowed me to "test drive" many of the activities and worksheets included in this book.

ABOUT THE AUTHOR

Tonia Caselman, Ph.D. is an Associate Professor in the School of Social Work at the University of Oklahoma - Tulsa. In addition to her teaching and research responsibilities, she maintains a private practice specializing in children and adolescents. She provides supervision and training for individuals and school programs. She previously worked as a school social worker in a private Catholic school. She is the author of *Impulse Control for Elementary Students, Impulse Control for Middle Schoolers, All About Boundaries* published by YouthLight, Inc. and *The Impulse Control Game* published by Franklin Learning Systems.

TABLE OF CONTENTS

TABLE OF CONTENTS
CONTINUED...

INTRODUCTION

> *"Tenderness and kindness are not signs of weakness and despair, but manifestations of strength and resolution."*
>
> *- Kahlil Gibran*

Empathy is the ability to understand what others feel and express that understanding in a caring way. It is considered the social emotion because it brings a sense of emotional connection to others. It has three important components: cognitive (perspective-taking), affective (emotional matching) and behavioral (displays of concern) (Vreeke & Van Der Mark, 2003). Empathy allows us to be affected or moved by another person; it is what allows us to be attuned to another so that we can gain a genuine sense of mutuality. When experiencing empathy we are receptive and open to the other person. Empathy moves us past the self and into relational awareness. It is this relational awareness that is not only basic to all healthy relationships, it is the root of prosocial behavior, altruism, kindness and peace.

Children begin to develop empathic concern for others between 1 and 2 years of age. Precursors of empathy begin as early as the first week of life when infants cry in response to the cries of other infants (Sagi & Hoffman, 1976). By 2 years of age children are quite able to identify others' general emotional states (Zahn-Waxler & Radke-Yarrow, 1990) and to engage in empathic behaviors (Zahn-Waxler & Radke-Yarrow, 1982). Indeed, many childcare workers can attest to the fact that very young children attempt to comfort distressed peers by bringing them toys or seeking the assistance of an adult.

Like most developmental domains, empathy increases with age. While a 2 year old may offer assistance to another, it is primarily based on her own needs rather than the needs of the person in distress. However, by age 6 or 7, a child is cognitively capable of "walking in someone else's shoes" and can, thereafter, increasingly engage in appropriate helping behavior. During peer interactions children learn to share, support, comfort and help – all aspects of empathy.

There are other determinants for empathic behaviors in children as well. Research has shown, for example, that empathic behavior is more likely to be elicited when a friend cries than when an acquaintance cries (Farver & Branstetter, 1994). Children are also more likely to engage in empathic behaviors when the receiver of their empathy is alone rather than with others (Farver & Branstetter, 1994). Finally, children with more positive temperaments and who are generally happier tend to exhibit more empathic/prosocial behaviors (Denham, 1998).

PURPOSE

Empathy, for the purposes of this book, is defined as the ability to perceive and understand the inner experience of another and to express that understanding through a supportive response. While researchers have identified two types of emotional responses to another's pain (one which shows a sympathetic reaction and one which shows a personal distress reaction), it is generally accepted that the sympathetic reaction is a more mature and functional type of empathy (eg. Denham, 1998). The ability to feel another's distress and then to focus on the other person rather than the self is the empathy style that motivates caring and compassionate behaviors (eg. Litvak-Miller & McDougall, 1997).

Teaching Children Empathy, The Social Emotion is designed to provide school social workers, psychologists, counselors and teachers with activities to help students think about and practice strategies to become more empathic or connected with others. Using a combination of cognitive-behavioral techniques and expressive techniques, it is intended to provide school personnel with tools to teach students how to recognize the feelings of others, how to allow themselves to share in those feelings and how to give thoughtful responses to others' feelings. The games, role-plays and worksheets described herein are presented in a playful, but thoughtful manner so that students can become easily engaged in the process of learning about and practicing empathy. The activities and discussions are designed to:

- Teach students the value of empathy
- Assist students in recognizing their own and others' feelings
- Help students put themselves in "someone else's shoes"
- Instruct students how to exhibit understanding and acceptance

RATIONALE

Research has shown that low levels of empathy are associated with children diagnosed with disruptive disorders (Wied, Goudena & Matthys, 2005) and with persons who display aggressive behaviors (eg. Feshbach, 1997; Kaukianen et. al., 1999). Indeed, empathy plays an important function in the inhibition of aggressive behavior and delinquency (Bandura, et. al., 2003). Higher levels of empathy have also been associated with self-esteem (Griffin-Shirley, & Nes, 2005), academic performance (Liff, 2003), forgiveness in relationships (Paleari, Regalia, & Fincham, 2005) and the development of prosocial behaviors (e.g. Denham & Burger, 1991; Eisenberg, McCreath, & Ahn, 1988; Staub, 1995). Both empathy and role-taking have been associated with imaginative thinking, a characteristic needed for creativity and humor (Strayer & Roberts, 1989). Certainly empathy is one of the most critical competencies for cognitive and social development (Attili, 1990).

Research supports empathy training as an effective means to enhance empathetic connections and increase prosocial behavior. Pecukonis (1990) found that four 1.5 hour empathy training sessions improved aggressive females' abilities to share vicariously in the emotional experiences of others. Salmon (2003) found that an intense empathy training program (two hours per day) with students in an alternative middle school and high school decreased suspensions, office referrals, school absences and the number of failing grades ('F's). In a program called "Second Step" which teaches elementary students empathy along with social skills, anger management and impulse control in 12 weekly sessions, students were found to exhibit fewer aggressive behaviors and more prosocial behaviors than a control group (Portner, 1997).

The idea for this book grew out of fifteen years of experience facilitating social skills groups. In working with children to make better connections with peers, it became clear that many children needed more than just concrete skills on how to join in, share, resolve conflicts, etc. They needed a recognition of others' feelings and the motivation to connect with those feelings in a way that made both parties feel closer. Finding very few resources on the topic, I began to study empathy and create games and worksheets for my groups. This book is an outgrowth of those efforts.

HOW TO USE THIS BOOK

Teaching Children Empathy, The Social Emotion can be easily used with students in grades K-6. Teachers, social workers, counselors, psychologists and other professional caregivers for children will find that the discussions and activities work best in small groups but they can also be modified and used in a larger classroom or in one-on-one counseling sessions. Activities can be altered to better suit each grade or developmental level.

Each chapter of this book is set up so that it covers a specific aspect of empathy development. All of the discussions and activities in a single chapter focus on that unique content. Lessons may be used as single sessions if only selected activities and worksheets are used. Or, lessons may be broken down into two or three lessons if all of the activities and worksheets are used. Generally, lessons should be kept to a 30-40 minute limit. Lessons are ordered so that they follow a progression or hierarchy of skills, but they may also be pulled out singly. Sections in each chapter include the object of the lesson, a rationale for the lesson, a list of needed supplies, a suggested way to introduce the topic, discussion questions, activities, and reproducible worksheets.

If those using this book would like to include information to parents, Appendix A includes a parent letter and a recommended reading list of children's books about empathy. The parent letter gives practical suggestions for reinforcing empathy development at home. Facilitators may also wish to use some of the recommended children's books for a periodic review or as a supplement to lessons.
.

PROCESS ESSENTIALS

While using the content of this book to teach empathy it is important that facilitators also pay attention to process components of the lessons. How we teach something is as important as what we teach. Here are some process essentials for helping children enhance their empathy:

CREATING A CARING GROUP.
Children are better learners when they feel safe and nurtured. Groups should be structured so that the emotional "climate" is warm and accepting. Facilitators should establish positive relationships with all of the students and students should be respectful, supportive and encouraging of one another. In order to establish this from the beginning, it may be necessary for the facilitator to set some "ground rules" before beginning the group. These can be negotiated among the group members or established by the facilitator. A few basic rules such as "no put-downs" and "everyone listens when someone is speaking" may be helpful in creating a safe and trusting group.

MODELING.

Facilitators should make every effort to model empathy. Social learning theory tells us that students will imitate our behavior. In addition, research shows that when empathy trainers (teachers, counselors, social workers, etc.) model empathic responses, children are more likely to take on these behaviors (Kremer & Dietzen, 1991). Facilitators should also exaggerate their use of feelings words so that children become accustomed to being sensitive to feelings.

REINFORCEMENT AND POSITIVE TRAIT ATTRIBUTION.

Be sure to give lots of recognition and praise (reinforcement) for small efforts at empathy. Catch students sharing, helping, verbalizing recognition of feelings and being kind to one another. Praise them in front of the group for the specific behavior and then emphasize that the reason that they exhibited this behavior is because it is in their nature to do so. Research has shown that reinforcing a particular internal trait increases the likelihood that children will replicate the behaviors congruent with that trait (Kohn, 1991). An example might be, "Uniqua, I liked how you helped Tiffany get a chair. You are really helpful."

FOCUS ON SIMILARITIES.

Research suggests that children's empathy is heightened when they perceive similarities between themselves and others (Black & Phillips, 1982). Facilitators can draw attention to similarities by verbalizing what they already know to be commonalities between group participants ("Susan, did you know that Carmetta also has an older sister at the high school?") or by verbalizing discoveries of commonalities during the course of the lessons ("It seems like Greg and Enricho both like to sit with one foot under them.").

PERSPECTIVE-TAKING.

Imagining another's point of view may be difficult for the group members so lots of practice is needed. Perspective-taking is essential in empathy development (e.g. Leith, & Baumeister, 1998; Schutte, et. al., 2001). Be sure to take time during lessons to ask students how someone else in the group might be feeling. This is particularly important if someone in the group hurts another's feelings. Rather than addressing this behavior as 'wrong' or 'bad,' ask the student how they think the behavior affected the other person or the group.

WHAT IS EMPATHY?

OBJECTIVES:

At the end of this lesson students will be able to:

- Define and describe the concept of empathy
- Differentiate empathic responses from nonempathic responses
- Identify the benefits of empathy

RATIONALE:

Many children will not have heard the term empathy. Having a name for a concept and understanding its meaning is an important first step to beginning a dialogue about the issue. Unless there is a definition of a term up-front, no two people can really talk about the same thing. Students need a clear understanding of the definition of empathy as well as examples of empathy in order to know what it is that they will be working on over the next few weeks. In defining empathy, students will also identify why empathy is an important life skill. Understanding the value of a skill helps to enhance engagement and motivation.

MATERIALS:

Biographies of famous empathic persons, poster boards or pieces of butcher paper, markers, masking tape, and newspaper and/or magazine stories

SCRIPT:

Can you think of a time that you got hurt and you went to your mother or grandmother or some other person because you knew that they would not only help you but would be sad with you? Well, that's empathy. Its about sharing feelings. Over the next few weeks we will be learning about empathy – what some people call the "social emotion." Empathy is actually the ability to read and understand another person's thoughts and feelings, and to let that person know in a positive way that you understand. Empathy helps us to have better relationships with others, to make good choices about our behavior and to feel positive about ourselves. The three (3) steps of empathy which we will be learning more about include:

- Recognize or "read" the other person's feelings
- Allow yourself to share in those feelings (feel them too)
- Give a supportive response (say or do something that lets the other person know you share their feelings)

DISCUSSION QUESTIONS:

- Can you think of time that you saw how someone was feeling and you said or did something that showed her/him that you cared?
- How do you think this person thought/felt about you showing empathy?
- How did you feel about yourself when you showed empathy?
- Why do you think that empathy is important?
- Who is the most empathic person you know? What does having empathy do for this person?

WHAT IS EMPATHY?

ACTIVITIES:

Activity 1. *Empathic People:* Study a famous empathic person. Studying the lives and achievements of famous empathetic persons increases children's desire to be like these people. Suggested persons might include Florence Nightingale, Martin Luther King, Jr., Albert Schweitzer, Mother Theresa, etc. Discuss how empathy made these persons lives richer.

Activity 2. *Empathy Week Advertisement:* Have students get into groups of 3-5 persons. Give each group a poster board or large piece of butcher paper and some markers. Tell the groups to pretend that their school will be having an Empathy Week and that they have been selected by the principal to create a poster to advertise it. Have each group share their poster; ask the other students to say what they like about it. Ask about how it feels to share your work with others and how it feels to receive compliments/encouragement for your work.

Activity 3. *Empathy Continuum:* Place a 6-8 foot piece of masking tape in a straight line on the floor. Explain to the students that one end represents extremely strong feelings of empathy (e.g. you can really understand what this person felt) and the other end represents no feelings of empathy at al (e.g. you really can't understand how this person felt); the middle of the line represents an average amount of empathy. Then read the following brief scenarios (feel free to think of others!) and ask the students to place themselves on the line based on how much they feel the feelings of the person in the scenario (empathy).

> **SCENARIO #A** – Raul is new at summer camp. He doesn't speak much English and no one is sitting with him at lunch.
> **SCENARIO #B** – Jessica is giving an oral book report in front of the class. She is getting mixed up and has a red face.
> **SCENARIO #C** – Tomomi is getting teased about being Japanese. The kids are saying that she only eats raw fish and sleeps on the floor.
> **SCENARIO #D** – Joe forgot his math homework and now the teacher is giving him a '0' for it. He looks like he might cry.
> **SCENARIO #E** – Maria's favorite uncle is in the military and he is getting ready to be stationed overseas in a dangerous location. She asked to go see the counselor to talk about it.

After the students have finished placing themselves on the empathy line for all of the scenarios, discuss their thoughts/reactions to the exercise. Ask questions such as: What do you think was the reason you felt more empathy for some of the children and less for others? Did it make a difference if the person in the situation was a boy or a girl? Did it make a difference if s/he was of a different culture? Did it make a difference if any of the situations had ever happened to you?

Activity 4. *Bringing Out Emotions:* Save newspaper and magazine stories of misfortune, suffering, deprivation, etc. and read these to the students (make sure that these are age-appropriate and not overly distressing). Research suggests that exposing people to emotionally arousing stimuli assists in encouraging empathetic feelings and responses (Pecukonis 1990). Discuss the students' reactions to these stories and ask what one could do to help.

WHAT IS EMPATHY?

✱ **Activity 5. *Empathic vs. Nonempathic Roleplay:*** Ask students to divide up into pairs. Ask each pair to role-play the same situation with two (2) different outcomes – one which demonstrates an empathic response and one which demonstrates a nonempathic response. Situations should show one student who is distressed (i.e. pet died, family is going to move, best friend is mad at her/him, etc.). In the first role-play the nondistressed student will try to cheer up the distressed student without first acknowledging the feeling. In the second role-play the nondistressed student will acknowledge the feeling of the distressed student and then say or do something supportive. Discuss with the audience why the second response is the better one. Have each pair perform their scenario.

REPRODUCIBLE WORKSHEETS:

Worksheet 1.1, *Definitions of Empathy,* challenges students to select a favorite definition of empathy from five (5) different definitions and to draw a picture of it. This exercise strengthens students' understanding of the meaning of empathy and allows them to personalize it in a kinesthetic manner.

Worksheet 1.2, *What Empathy Looks Like,* asks students to differentiate between comic figures' empathic thoughts/statements and nonempathic thoughts/statements. Additionally, it asks students to explain how the empathic figures are indeed exhibiting empathy. This worksheet helps students identify behaviors which are empathic and helps them to realize that nonempathic responses can appear selfish and/or insensitive.

Worksheet 1.3, *Empathy Grade Card,* asks students to "grade" themselves in the areas of asking about others' feelings, reading facial expressions and voice tone, making sympathetic and congratulatory statements to others, putting oneself in others' shoes, doing nice things and seeing others' point of view.

Worksheet 1.4, *World without Empathy,* challenges students to imagine what their lives would be like if people did not show empathy to one another. It asks them to respond to questions regarding families, the classroom, the playground and traffic on the streets. This worksheet assists students in recognizing the importance of empathy in everyday life.

Worksheet 1.5, *The Secret of Success,* asks students to discover a message by Henry Ford by using a numeric code at the bottom of the page. The secret message is, "If there is any secret of success, it lies in the ability to get the other person's point of view and see things from his angle as well as from your own." Discuss with the students what they think this means. This worksheet helps students see that very successful people identify empathy as a source of their success.

DEFINITIONS OF EMPATHY

DIRECTIONS: *Listed below are several definitions of empathy. Circle the one that you like the most and then draw a picture below of yourself showing this to another person.*

1. The ability to "put yourself in someone else's shoes"

2. The ability to understand other people's feelings even though your feelings are different

3. The ability to be sensitive to others' feelings

4. The ability to experience other people's feelings

5. The ability to show caring behaviors towards others

THIS IS ME SHOWING EMPATHY

WHAT EMPATHY LOOKS LIKE
(AND DOESN'T LOOK LIKE!)

DIRECTIONS: *Look at the children below. Decide which ones are considering other people's feelings and which ones are not. Write the names of the empathic people at the bottom of the page. Then write why you think they are showing empathy.*

List the names of the people who are showing empathy and how they are doing it:

_____ : _____

_____ : _____

_____ : _____

EMPATHY GRADE CARD

DIRECTIONS: *Put an X in a box to the right of each statement that best describes how well you do each one.*

	EXCELLENT	GOOD	SO-SO	POOR
I ask people about their feelings				
I can tell what other people are feeling by the look on their face.				
I can tell what other people are feeling by the tone of their voice.				
I try to help people feel better when I see that they are sad.				
I congratulate others on their successes.				
I can "put myself in someone else's shoes."				
I like to do nice things for others.				
I like to hear others' point of view.				

WORLD WITHOUT EMPATHY

DIRECTIONS: *Imagine (but only for a short time because it's not a pleasant thought!) what the world might be like if people didn't have empathy for one another. Answer the following questions:*

1. What might happen if there was no empathy in families?

    _____

    _____

    _____

2. What might happen if there was no empathy in the classroom?

    _____

    _____

    _____

3. What might happen if there was no empathy on the playground?

    _____

    _____

    _____

4. What might happen if there was no empathy driving on the streets?

    _____

    _____

    _____

5. Would you want to live in a world without empathy? Why or why not?

    _____

    _____

    _____

THE SECRET OF SUCCESS*

*Created by Henry Ford, founder of Ford Motors and developer of moving assembly belts which made cars affordable to the average American.

DIRECTIONS: Using the Message Decoder at the bottom of the page, fill in the blanks and find out what Henry Ford said about empathy.

"

``9 6``   ``19 8 5 17 5``   ``9 18``   ``1 14 23``   ``15 14 5``   ``18 5 3 17 5 19``

``19 15``   ``18 20 3 3 5 18 18``   ``,``   ``9 19``   ``12 9 5 18``   ``9 14``   ``19 8 5``

``1 2 9 12 9 19 23``   ``19 15``   ``7 5 19``   ``19 8 5``   ``15 19 8 5 17``

``,``   ``16 5 17 18 15 14``   ``18``   ``16 15 9 14 19``   ``15 6``   ``21 9 5 22``   ``1 14 4``

``18 5 5``   ``19 8 9 14 7 18``   ``6 17 15 13``   ``8 9 18``   ``1 14 7 12 5``

``1 18``   ``22 5 12 12``   ``1 18``   ``23 15 20 17 18``. "

1	2	3	4	5	6	7	8	9	10	11	12	13	14	15	16	17	18	19	20	21	22	23
A	B	C	D	E	F	G	H	I	J	K	L	M	N	O	P	R	S	T	U	V	W	Y

EMPATHY STARTS WITH KNOWING YOUR OWN FEELINGS

OBJECTIVES:

At the end of this lesson students will be able to:

- Name several feeling words and know their meanings
- Use feeling words to describe their own internal states
- Determine levels of various feelings
- Associate particular feelings with particular situations

RATIONALE:

When enhancing students' empathy, it is helpful to have them first get in touch with their own feelings (Black and Phillips 1982). But identifying feelings can be confusing. Students may know that they are feeling something (often they may limit these descriptions to feeling "good" or feeling "bad") but not know how to articulate those feelings. Assisting students in identifying their own feeling states will help them to better understand the feelings of others (Eisenberg et al., 1993). Research has shown that when adults present children with words to describe internal emotional states children show increased knowledge of their own feelings and increased sensitivity to others' feelings (Fabes, Eisenberg & Miller, 1990). Understanding one's own emotional life also contributes to emotional regulation which is needed in empathy development.

MATERIALS:

Several copies of Appendix B, pencils, paper, crayons or markers, Jenga-type building blocks, glue, various recorded instrumental pieces of music, and a tape player or CD player.

SCRIPT:

Today we are going to talk about your feelings. Everyone has feelings – they are quite normal. Sometimes it is helpful to talk about feelings so it is important that you have words to describe them. Some feeling words that you may already know are happy, sad, angry, scared, shy, embarrassed, confused, and silly – and there are lots of others! You can know your feelings by paying attention to your body. For example, when you are angry you may feel your jaw get tight or feel your hands make a fist or feel your heart beat faster. When you are sad you may feel your head and shoulders sagging or feel your eyes fill up with tears or feel yourself moving in slow motion. It's also important to know what makes us feel certain feelings. For example, being teased may make you feel sad or angry; getting a good grade may make you feel relieved or proud. Let's talk some more about feelings!

DISCUSSION QUESTIONS:

- What are some feelings that you have had? Which of these feelings do you like to have and which ones do you not like to have?
- Which feelings make you feel strong? Which feelings make you feel weak?
- What things make you feel happy? What things make you feel sad? What things make you feel scared?
- Do you ever talk about your feelings? Who do you talk to about them?

EMPATHY STARTS WITH KNOWING YOUR OWN FEELINGS

ACTIVITIES:

Activity 1. *My Feelings Today:* Distribute copies of the feeling words sheet in Appendix B. Instruct students to sit in a circle. Ask them to identify two (2) feelings that they have had today and the situations that prompted those feelings. Remind students to be good listeners.

Activity 2. *Guess a Feeling:* Ask students to break up into groups of three (3) persons. Direct one of the students to write down a feeling word on a small piece of paper. Then have the other two (2) students attempt to guess what the feeling is by each asking 3-5 questions about the feeling (i.e. "Would I feel this feeling if …." Or "Is this a feeling that I would like to have?" etc.). When the feeling has been revealed, allow the other students in the group to write down a feeling word and repeat the process.

Activity 3. *Feelings Jenga®:* Using an inexpensive Jenga® type game, write feeling words on each of the blocks. Appendix B has a list of feeling words that can be used (or feel free to use any others that are important to your group). Then stack the blocks and begin playing like the traditional Jenga game – only this time, when students pull out a block, they must read the feeling word on it and share a time when they felt that feeling. Continue playing until the tower falls.

Activity 4. *Levels of Feelings:* Have students differentiate varying degrees of a particular feeling by asking them to show with their bodies "a little <feeling word>," "a medium amount of <feeling word>," and "a lot of <feeling word>." For older students you can use specific words that describe these degrees of feelings (i.e. frustrated/angry/enraged or nervous/scared/terrified or content/happy/excited, etc.).

Activity 5. *The Feelings-Body Connection:* Ask students to stand. Instruct them to follow a set of verbal directions to create specific facial expressions, gestures, movements and body positions. When the instructions for each set is complete, give students permission to call out the emotion that is connected with those physical sensations.

- **SET 1:** Slump your shoulders. Hang your head. Turn the corners of your mouth down. Make your eye brows frown. Make your body feel heavy. Move slowly. (sad)
- **SET 2:** Put your hand on your stomach. Wrinkle your nose. Stick your tongue out so that it is flat. Turn the corners of your mouth down. (disgusted)
- **SET 3:** Stand up really straight. Turn the corners of your mouth up. Make you body feel light. Walk with a "bounce" in your step. (happy)
- **SET 4:** Squint your eyes. Clench your teeth. Make your muscles tight all over your body. Make your hands into fists. (angry)
- **SET 5:** Open up your eyes really wide. Raise your eyebrows. Smile. Freeze your body but move your head backwards. (surprise)
- **SET 6:** Close your eyes. Make your muscles tight. Draw your arms and hands up close to your chest. Shake a little. (scared)

EMPATHY STARTS WITH KNOWING YOUR OWN FEELINGS

Activity 6. *Feelings and Music:* Distribute copies of the feeling words sheet in Appendix B. Then explain how emotions can be felt in music. Select several varied instrumental pieces of music and have the students listen to short excerpts from them. Direct the students to call out emotions that they feel in the music. Most instrumental pieces will work for this exercise but some classical suggestions include Robert Schumann's Perfect Happiness, Mahler's Symphony No 11. III, Funeral March, the 4th movement of Tchaikovsky's Symphony No. 4, the 3rd movement of G. Mahler's Symphony No. 6 & Chopin's Prelude in E Minor Op. 28.

Activity 7. *A Feelings Song:* Create and sing multiple feelings verses of the song, "If you're happy and you know it…" For example:

- If you're happy and you know it, shake a hand – (shake, shake)

- If you're sad and you know it, shed a tear – ("boo-hoo")

- If you're mad and you know it, use your words – ("I'm mad")

- If you're confused and you know it, scratch your head – (scratch, scratch)

- If you're silly and you know it, make a face – ( )

REPRODUCIBLE WORKSHEETS:

Worksheet 2.1, *The Color of Feelings,* asks students to associate different colors with different feeling words. This allows students a nonverbal experience with various feeling words. It allows them to get a "feel" for feelings.

Worksheet 2.2, *Feelings Word Search,* asks students to find different feeling words. This worksheet continues to familiarize them with a feeling words vocabulary to better express themselves and, ultimately, to better understand others.

Worksheet 2.3, *How Would You Feel?,* presents students with diverse situations where they are asked to identify how they would feel if the situation were to happen to them. Associating feelings with events and triggers is an important part of emotional literacy. It also prepares students for recognizing what kinds of events might produce certain feelings in others.

Worksheet 2.4, *Matching Feelings,* asks students to find feeling matches among different feeling words. This sheet exposes students to additional words to describe feeling states and helps them to recognize that similar feelings can be expressed differently.

Worksheet 2.5, *Feelings Families,* instructs students to group various feeling words into similar groups or "families." This task helps students to realize that there are different levels of feelings as well as nuances to feelings.

THE COLOR OF FEELINGS

DIRECTIONS: *People develop empathy by recognizing and understanding their own feelings. After understanding our own feelings we can understand the feelings of others. Look at the feeling words below and then think about what color each feeling reminds you of. Color the shapes the color that reminds you of the feeling.*

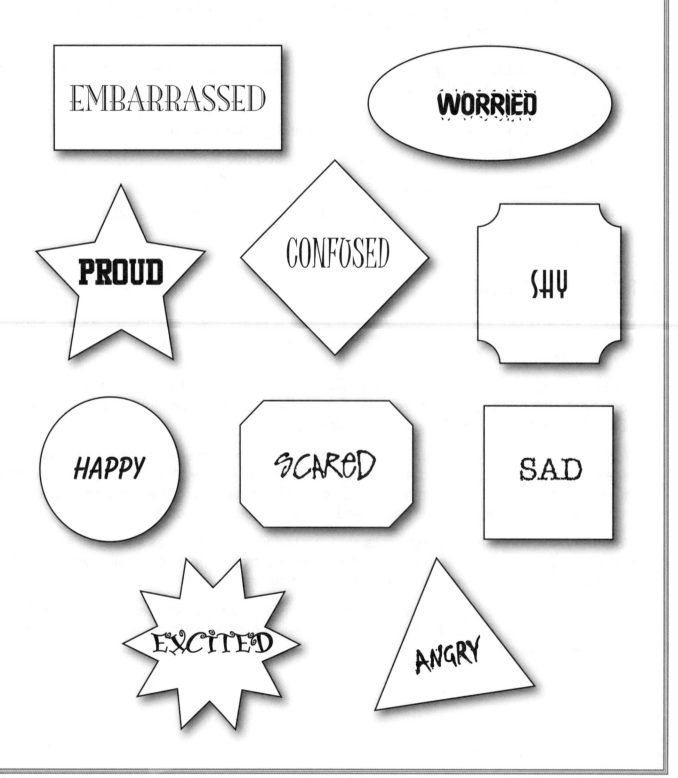

FEELINGS WORD SEARCH

DIRECTIONS: *Find the following words in the puzzle below.*

CONFUSED	JEALOUS	ANGRY	EXCITED	HAPPY
HOPEFUL	WORRIED	SCARED	IRRITATED	SAD

```
N  Q  C  B  E  O  F  M  X  V  Y  W  L  Z  U  D
F  F  S  R  N  N  A  L  C  H  R  G  V  R  A  Q
A  W  K  P  T  K  Z  W  O  R  R  I  E  D  X  E
P  A  N  L  V  O  U  A  N  G  R  Y  W  X  T  D
K  J  Z  Q  H  O  P  E  F  U  L  T  Z  Q  N  H
C  O  I  P  H  X  B  R  U  H  Z  E  D  A  K  K
N  G  R  L  P  P  J  U  S  C  A  R  E  D  V  K
E  I  R  C  Y  U  Q  C  E  V  D  P  B  H  K  U
H  Y  I  P  F  Y  A  M  D  U  F  J  P  O  E  W
E  P  T  X  Z  H  V  F  J  I  X  T  A  Y  R  T
J  E  A  L  O  U  S  J  U  N  H  L  X  J  B  X
A  Y  T  J  Q  A  G  A  L  P  W  Z  T  E  R  A
N  N  E  X  C  I  T  E  D  L  G  S  Y  R  O  E
E  D  D  L  L  E  Z  Z  C  L  Y  A  K  B  H  M
H  S  P  T  O  P  Y  E  U  L  H  C  W  I  B  G
B  R  O  C  P  C  P  E  I  A  F  L  T  N  F  F
```

HOW WOULD YOU FEEL?

DIRECTIONS: *Listed below are some feeling words. Use them or think of other feeling words to describe how you might feel in the following situations. Write the feeling word(s) that you would feel after each situation. Don't worry if your feelings are different from someone else's feelings.*

FEELING WORDS

happy	sad	angry	excited	confused
silly	worried	jealous	nervous	embarrassed
guilty	shy	bored	frustrated	careful

1. Your parents just told you that your family will be moving.

_____

2. Your teacher just blamed you for something you didn't do.

_____

3. The doctor just told you that you need an operation.

_____

4. You got caught sneaking a cookie before dinner.

_____

5. You missed several days of school and now your class is doing something new in math.

_____

6. Your sister took something of yours without asking to borrow it.

_____

7. You have a big social studies test today and you didn't study very much for it.

_____

MATCHING FEELINGS

DIRECTIONS: *There are often several ways to describe a feeling. Find the feelings that are similar in each column. Draw a line connecting them. Example: HAPPY is similar to CHEERFUL.*

HAPPY	**MAD**
SAD	**ASHAMED**
SURE	**CONFIDENT**
ANGRY	**SHOCKED**
SCARED	**PERPLEXED**
SURPRISED	**TIMID**
GUILTY	**THRILLED**
SHY	**GLOOMY**
LONELY	**PLAYFUL**
BORED	**AFRAID**
EXCITED	**DULL**
CONFUSED	**CHEERFUL**
SILLY	**LONESOME**

FEELINGS FAMILIES

DIRECTIONS: *Feelings can often times be grouped together because they are similar – kind of like families. Look at the feelings word bank below and then write each feeling word in the family you think it belongs to.*

FEELINGS WORD BANK			
glad	tearful	mad	annoyed
depressed	hopeless	pleased	fearful
furious	frightened	cheerful	worried
excited	irritated	afraid	lonely

HAPPY FAMILY

SCARED FAMILY

ANGRY FAMILY

SAD FAMILY

EMPATHY & LEARNING TO READ OTHERS' FEELINGS

OBJECTIVES:

At the end of this lesson students will be able to:

- Understand the importance of reading nonverbal communication
- Identify feelings on others' facial expressions
- Identify feelings from others' voice tones
- Name other's likely feelings based on various situations

RATIONALE:

Before students can attune themselves to others' feelings they must first be able to detect and "read" what those other persons' feelings are. It is also impossible to know what to say or do for others if students don't know how those others feel. Knowing whether another person is sad, angry, proud or nervous makes a big difference in how one responds. Reading others' feelings is the first step in empathy development.

MATERIALS:

Pictures of feeling faces cut out from magazines, a hat or small box, a TV with video or DVD player, video recording of a segment from a TV show or movie, index cards, a marker, bulletin board pins, slices of bread, peanut butter and/or cream cheese, raisins, sunflower seeds, thin red and black licorice, plastic knives, paper plates, napkins, modeling clay and one (1) copy of Appendix C.

SCRIPT:

Did you know that over 60% of communication is nonverbal – or based on body language? That means that we "talk" to one another with our bodies and our faces. Just like you have learned to read books you can learn to read other people, too. For example, imagine that you are new to your school. As the teacher introduces you to other students, one student says, "Nice to meet you" while looking at his book and frowning. The next student says "Nice to meet you" while looking you in the eye and smiling. Both students have said the same words but which student seems genuinely happy to meet you? How did you know this? The ability to read other people's feelings is an important part of developing empathy.

DISCUSSION QUESTIONS:

- What are some reasons that we need to be able to read others' feelings?
- Have you ever been able to read someone's feelings without that person even saying a word? When?
- Has anyone ever been able to read your feelings without you even saying a word? How did that feel?
- How do you know if someone is sad? Mad? Happy? Scared? What does their face look like? What does their body look like? What does their voice sound like?

EMPATHY & LEARNING TO READ OTHERS' FEELINGS

ACTIVITIES:

Activity 1. *Musical Feelings Faces:* Cut out various feeling faces from newspapers, magazines, comic books, etc. and place them in a hat or small box. Instruct students to sit in a circle as you pass the hat around while music is playing. When the music stops, the student holding the hat puts her/his hand in the hat, pulls out a feeling picture, identifies the emotion that is represented and makes a guess about what could have happened to the person to have caused the feeling.

Activity 2. *Silent Movie Feelings:* Videotape a movie or TV show segment prior to meeting with the students. Preferably choose something that the students have not seen before. Then show the tape/DVD with the sound turned off. Ask students what they think are the thoughts and feelings of the characters. Pause the tape from time to time and ask the students what they think is going on.

Activity 3. *Finding Feelings:* Cut out various feeling faces from magazines, newspapers, comic books, etc. On several index cards write down one different feeling word per card (i.e. happy, sad, angry, scared, excited, silly, bored, shy, etc.). Make sure that there is a feeling word for each feeling that is represented on a picture. Pin the pictures to the wall around the room. Hand each student an index card with a feeling word and ask the students to find and stand by the face that matches the feeling word that is named on their card. After everyone has found their feeling face, collect the cards, shuffle, redistribute among the students and play again.

Activity 4. *Edible Feelings Faces:* Ask students to sit at a table with a paper plate, a slice of bread, and plastic knife. In the center of the table place containers of peanut butter (or cream cheese for those students who are allergic to peanut butter), raisins, sunflower seeds, and thin red and black licorice cut into various lengths. Hand each student a slice of bread and a plastic knife and instruct them to spread either the peanut butter or the cream cheese onto the bread. Then explain that they will use the other ingredients to create a feeling face on the slice of bread. Remind them to consider how mouths, eyes, eyebrows, etc. look for the feeling that they are creating. After "faces" are completed, ask students to show their creations to the other students and then invite them to eat them.

Activity 5. *Molding Feelings:* Direct students to break up into pairs. Ask one of the students in each pair to tell of an experience that s/he has had recently. Hand the other student in the pair some modeling clay and ask her/him to mold it into their partner to show with the face and body how that experience felt. Allow the partners to switch so that both students get an opportunity to tell their story and to use the modeling clay.

Activity 6. *Feelings by Voice:* Explain to the students that people sometimes say one thing but mean another. This can often be detected in voice tone. Then read the following items (using the voice tone that is italicized) and ask students to identify the true feeling of the person who might be saying such a thing.

- "I suppose now that you have that new fat girl for a friend you won't want me as your friend anymore. I don't really care, but I'd be embarrassed if I were you to be seen with her." Does this person feel excited, jealous or confused? How do you know that?

EMPATHY & LEARNING TO READ OTHERS' FEELINGS

- "Don't laugh at me, you idiot! Its not my fault that I slipped! The stupid janitor put too much wax on the floor! Does this person feel depressed, hopeless or embarrassed? How do you know that?
- "I don't care that I had to miss the championship game because I got sick. I'm sure that it wasn't that much fun anyway." Does this person feel disappointed, content or happy? How do you know that?
- "I hate school! The teachers give me too much work and then I have to come home and do all my homework and chores around the house. I feel like I'll never get it all done!" Does this person feel relief, pressured or angry? How do you know that?
- "My hamster died last night but its OK. I'll probably get another one. I'm kind of tired today but its probably because I didn't get much sleep last night." Does this person feel satisfied, careful or sad? How do you know that?

Activity 7. *Listening for Feelings:* Turn your back to the students and read the nonsense words/phrases in Appendix C in various tones of voice (i.e. happy, sad, angry, scared, confused, bored, etc.). (Having your back to the students does not allow them to read your facial expression, thereby forcing them to attend to voice quality only.) Have the students call out the feeling that matches your voice tone. A variation of this exercise is to make copies of nonsense words/phrases and allow the students to read them to one another using different tones of voice.

REPRODUCIBLE WORKSHEETS:

Worksheet 3.1, *Create and Read a Face,* allows students to create their own feeling face by cutting and pasting face parts on a blank face. After creating their feeling faces, students can show their work and have other students try to guess the feeling that they have created. This activity helps students to better understand the specific facial parts that express various feelings.

Worksheet 3.2, *Bubbles of Emotions,* asks students to draw lines between matching feelings faces. This activity allows students to differentiate various facial expressions that portray feelings.

Worksheet 3.3, *Feelings Crossword,* requires students to read feeling faces and then print the corresponding feeling word inside of a crossword puzzle. This worksheet continues to familiarize students with different facial expressions that typify feeling states.

Worksheet 3.4, *Reading Body Language,* asks students to identify the feelings of several bodies without facial cues. While faces offer the most information regarding feelings, it is helpful to understand body language in its entirety. This exercise expands students' abilities to read body cues for feelings.

Worksheet 3.5, *How do Others Feel?,* asks students to consider four (4) typical childhood events (positive and negative) which are written inside of boxes. Each event is surrounded by several feelings words. Students are asked to identify multiple feelings for each situation. This worksheet allows students the opportunity for perspective-taking while considering how various events affect feelings.

CREATE & READ A FACE

DIRECTIONS: *Cut out a set of eyes, a nose, and a mouth below and glue them on the blank face. Try to create a particular feeling. When you are finished, share your newly created face with others. See if you can guess what feelings each others' faces show!*

28

BUBBLES OF EMOTION

DIRECTIONS: *Inside each of the "bubbles" below there are several faces of the same person showing various emotions. Draw a line between the matching feeling faces within each circle (or "bubble").*

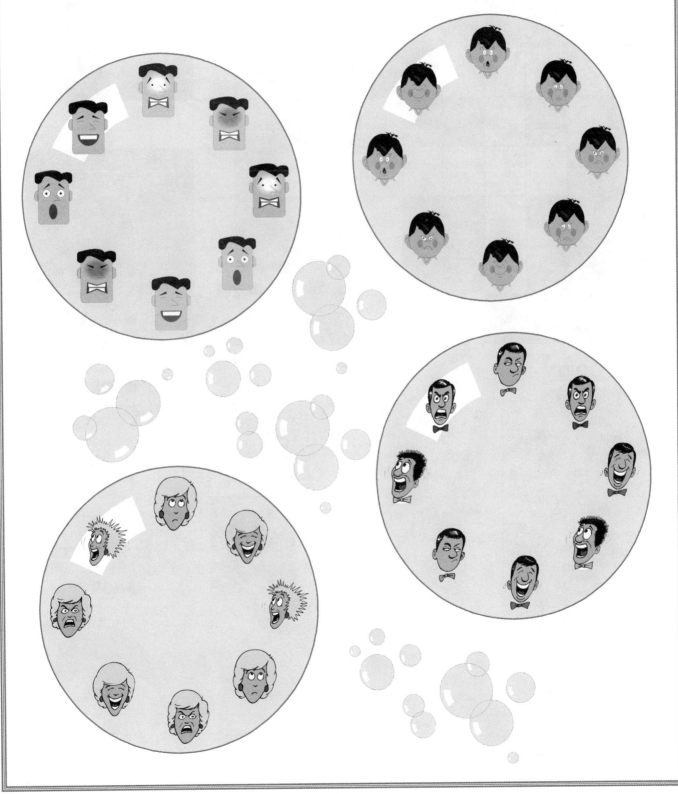

FEELINGS CROSSWORD

DIRECTIONS: Using the feeling words listed in the WORD BANK, "read" the feeling faces below and write in the feeling word in the numbered spaces either across or down on the crossword puzzle.

DOWN

1.

2.

3.

4.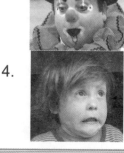

ACROSS

1.

2.

3.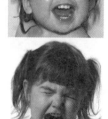

4.

5.

WORD BANK

WORRIED

HAPPY

SCARED

CONFUSED

ANGRY

PROUD

SHY

SAD

SILLY

READING BODY LANGUAGE

DIRECTIONS: *Look at the body postures and gestures on the left. On the lines next to each figure, write down what you think the person is feeling or thinking.*

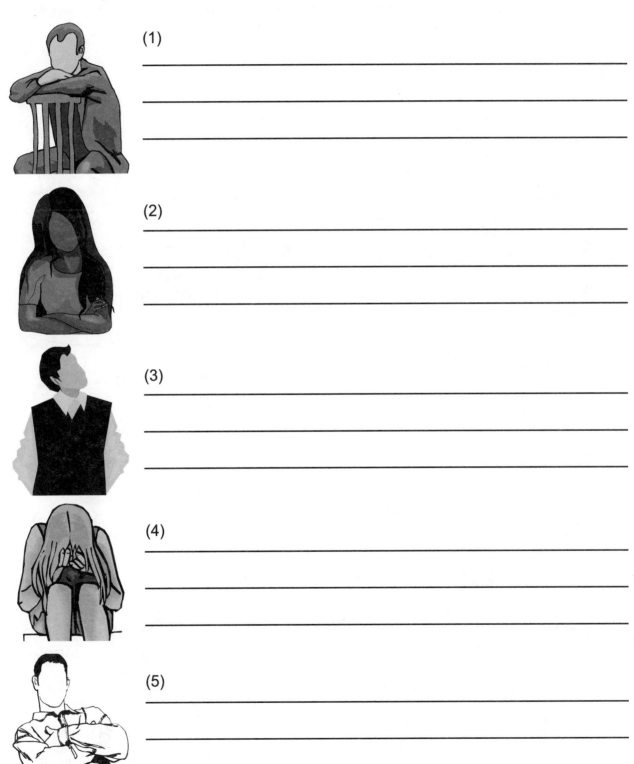

(1)
_____
_____
_____

(2)
_____
_____
_____

(3)
_____
_____
_____

(4)
_____
_____
_____

(5)
_____
_____
_____

HOW DO OTHERS FEEL?

DIRECTIONS: *In each of the flowers below, there is a situation written in the center with feeling words in the petals around it. Draw lines from the situation to the feelings that you think are produced by the situation. In other words, how would someone feel if the situation were happening to them?*

EMPATHY THROUGH LISTENING

OBJECTIVES:

At the end of this lesson students will be able to:

- Name specific skills of active listening
- Understand how listening (or not listening) creates emotions in others
- Paraphrase and reflect feelings from listening

RATIONALE:

Carl Rogers suggested that empathy involves deep, reflective listening (Rogers, 1951). Certainly listening communicates value and respect to the speaker and promotes understanding and trust between people. Being listened to gives us a sense of being taken seriously; that our thoughts and feelings matter to others. Michael Nichols in his book, Are You Listening, states that it is a human condition that we all yearn to be listened to and understood in order to escape our separateness. Listening is an important avenue in which empathy and genuine human connection can be expressed and developed. Assisting students in developing genuine, reflective listening skills will enhance their empathy development.

MATERIALS:

Paper, crayons/markers, index cards and a toy microphone (optional)

SCRIPT:

Do you know the difference between hearing and listening? <wait for student responses> Hearing is something that our ears do, but listening requires ours ears and our brain. Listening means that you think about what the person is saying. You really pay attention and show that you are interested. You try to understand how the other person feels and thinks. Most people aren't really very good at listening – they just take turns speaking – but being a generous listener can help you to learn more and to be well-liked. Good listeners do the following:

- Look at the speaker
- Lean forward and nod your head
- Think about the words and the feelings of the speaker
- Match facial expressions to the feelings of the speaker
- Show an interest by asking questions

DISCUSSION QUESTIONS:

- How do you feel when someone really listens to you? How do you think you make others feel if you really listen to them?
- How do you feel when someone doesn't listen to you? How do you think you make others feel if you don't listen to them?
- When is it hard to be a good listener? When is it easy to be a good listener?
- Who do you know is a good listener? How can you tell that s/he is a good listener?
- What are some other reasons that it is important to be a good listener?

EMPATHY THROUGH LISTENING

ACTIVITIES:

Activity 1. *Two Mouths and One Ear:* Share the quotation by Mark Twain, "If we were supposed to talk more than we listen, we would have two mouths and one ear." Ask students what they think this means. Then instruct them to draw pictures of a person with two (2) mouths and one (1) ear. Have each student share their picture and discuss how this body type might be problematic in day-to-day life (i.e. more talking and less listening).

Activity 2. *Active Listening Practice:* Divide students into pairs. Ask one member of the pair to be the speaker and the other member to be the listener. Have the listener practice the five (5) steps of active listening (look at the speaker, lean forward and nod your head, think about the words and the feelings of the speaker, match your facial expression to the feelings of the speaker, and show an interest by asking questions) while the speaker describes something of interest. After a few minutes, ask the speaker to gently critique the listener's listening skills. Be sure to encourage students to give constructive feedback. Some questions that you can use for the feedback include:

- Did the listener look at you?
- Did the listener lean forward?
- Did the listener nod her/his head to show s/he was listening?
- Did it seem like the listener was thinking about what you were saying?
- Did you feel like the listener was interested in what you had to say? Why or why not?
- Did the listener ask questions about what you were talking about?
- What was the listener's best skill? What does the listener need to work on?

Activity 3. *Talk Show Host:* Have two (2) students volunteer to play "Talk Show Host." Most children are familiar with television programs where a host interviews a guest. Have one of the students play the "host" and the other play the "guest." Direct the "host" to show great interest in the guest by asking interview questions that build on previous statements that the "guest" has made. Be sure that the "host" understands that s/he is not to simply ask random questions but is to carefully listen to the "guest's" remarks and to further explore those remarks by asking relevant questions. A toy microphone can be a fun (but optional!) prop.

Activity 4. *Paraphrasing:* Explain to the students the listening concept of paraphrasing (rephrasing/restating the content of what has been said). Describe how paraphrasing shows the speaker that you are really thinking about what s/he is saying. Explain that paraphrasing sometimes starts with phrases like, "It sounds like…," "It seems like…," "So you…," "I guess that…," "I hear you saying…," "I understand that…," etc.

Example: "You just don't understand what it's like to have to sit and wait for my mother to get off the phone just so I can ask permission to go outside! Sometimes I just feel like going out anyway." Paraphrase, "It sounds like you really want to go outside and it's hard to wait for permission."

Read the following statements one at a time and ask the students to paraphrase them.

a. *"My mom is so busy feeding and diapering and playing with the baby that she can't help me with my homework. I don't know how to do this new math!"*

EMPATHY THROUGH LISTENING

b. *"My mom and dad are getting a divorce so my brother and I have to go back and forth between their two houses every week. It stinks."*

c. *"These new guys in my neighborhood know how to do all kinds of tricks on their bicycles. They said that they would teach me if I come outside more."*

d. *"Sally plays with me one day and ignores me the next. I never really know if she likes me or not."*

e. *"Everyone on my soccer team just goofs around and never takes practice seriously. How are we ever supposed to win if we don't practice hard?"*

Activity 5. *Reflecting Feelings:* Explain to the students the listening concept of reflecting feelings (listening for the emotional tone of what the speaker is saying and putting a feeling word to it). Describe how reflecting feelings shows the speaker that you really understand him/her. Explain that reflecting feelings sometimes starts with phrases like, "You must really feel…," "You sound …," "Are you feeling…," "I bet you are…," "You seem…," etc.

Example: "You just don't understand what it's like to have to sit and wait for my mother to get off the phone just so I can ask permission to go outside! Sometimes I just feel like going out anyway." Reflecting feeling, "You seem pretty frustrated."

Read the statements again in activity number 4 (above) and ask the students to make a reflecting feeling response.

Activity 6. *Famous Quotations:* Prior to meeting with the students, write the following listening quotations on index cards (one quotation per card). Mix these up and then ask students to select one and sit in a group. Have each student read their quotation and then ask the group what they think it means. Other quotations can certainly be used as well!

- *"Every person in this life has something to teach me -- and as soon as I accept that, I open myself to truly listening."* -- Catherine Doucette

- *"A good listener is not only popular everywhere, but after a while he knows something."* -- Wilson Mizner

- *"The principle of listening, someone has said, is to develop a big ear rather than a big mouth."* -- Howard G. and Jeanne Hendricks

- *"Listening is an attitude of the heart, a genuine desire to be with another."* -- J. Isham

- *"The friends who listen to us are the ones we move toward."* -- Karl Menninger

- *"Seek first to understand, and then to be understood."* -- Stephen Covey

- *"One of the hardest things to do in life is to listen without intent to reply."* --Source Unknown

- *"The greatest compliment that was ever paid me was when one asked me what I thought, and attended to my answer."* -- Henry David Thoreau

- *"Good listeners, like precious gems, are to be treasured."* -- Walter Anderson

- *"An open ear is the only believable sign of an open heart."* -- David Augsburger

- *"Hearing is a faculty; listening is an art."* -- Source Unknown

- *"You can't fake listening. It shows."* -- Raquel Welch

EMPATHY THROUGH LISTENING

REPRODUCIBLE WORKSHEETS:

Worksheet 4.1, *Roadblocks to Empathic Listening,* helps students to recognize some of the problems that they may encounter as they try to be empathic listeners. Some of these obstacles include getting distracted, changing the subject, finishing the speaker's sentences, wanting to give advise, making a joke out of what the speaker said, planning what to say next, and believing that you are right. This worksheet asks the students to identify three (3) obstacles that they have the most trouble with and to come up with a plan for removing those obstacles in their lives.

Worksheet 4.2, *Empathic Listening Helps Others to Feel Great,* is a word scramble that lists five (5) feelings that are produced when people are on the receiving end of empathic listening (happy, loved, special, important and respected). This activity helps students recognize that empathic listening produces enjoyable emotional effects for others.

Worksheet 4.3, *Finding Empathic Listeners,* asks students to identify which scenes display empathic listening. This worksheet reinforces the behavioral, observable aspects of empathic listening and reminds students that making eye contact, leaning forward, looking interested, etc. are important listening skills.

Worksheet 4.4, *Empathic Listening Statements,* lists both empathic and self-focused verbal responses to others. Students are asked to write the empathic statements inside a picture of an ear. Reproducing (through writing) kind and thoughtful statements allows students continued practice in empathic responding.

Worksheet 4.5, *Rating Your Empathic Listening,* instructs students to evaluate themselves as either excellent, good, fair or poor on ten (10) behavioral, affective and motivational characteristics of empathic listening. Students then identify a strength and a weakness from the different facets of empathic listening. This activity assists students in examining their own personal empathic listening skills, thereby applying what they have learned about empathic listening to themselves.

ROADBLOCKS TO EMPATHIC LISTENING

Directions: *There are lots of "roadblocks" (things that get in the way) to empathic listening. Look at the list of behaviors that get in the way of empathic listening on the left. Decide which three (3) you have the most trouble with and write those on the roadblock signs on the right. Then answer the question below.*

- **Getting distracted**

- **Changing the subject**

- **Finishing the speaker's sentences**

- **Daydreaming**

- **Wanting to give advice**

- **Making a joke out of what the speaker says**

- **Remembering your own experiences with what the speaker is talking about**

- **Thinking that what the person says is stupid or boring**

- **Planning what to say next**

- **Believing that you are right**

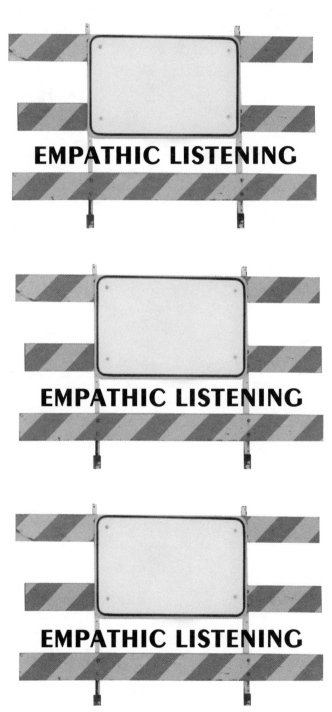

What is your plan for taking these roadblocks out of the way of your empathic listening?

_____

EMPATHIC LISTENING HELPS OTHERS TO FEEL GREAT

Directions: *People love to feel heard – and they feel heard when we listen with empathy. In fact, listening with empathy makes people feel great about themselves and their listeners. See if you can discover some of the other feelings that are produced when we are empathic listeners. Unscramble the words below for feeling words that describe how it feels to be heard (HINT: all of the words start with the first letter that is listed).*

H P A P Y

— — — — —

L D V E O

— — — — —

S L E C I P A

— — — — — — —

I T O R A N T M P

— — — — — — — — —

R S E E E C T D P

— — — — — — — — —

FINDING EMPATHIC LISTENERS

Directions: *Look at the pictures below. Some show examples of empathic listening and some do not. Draw hearts around the examples of empathic listening and write the word, "OOPS" on top of the poor listening.*

EMPATHIC LISTENING STATEMENTS

Directions: *Sometimes we need to communicate to others that we are being empathic listeners. This means that we need to respond with statements that show we care and want to listen even more. Look at the statements below. Write the empathic listening statements inside the ear.*

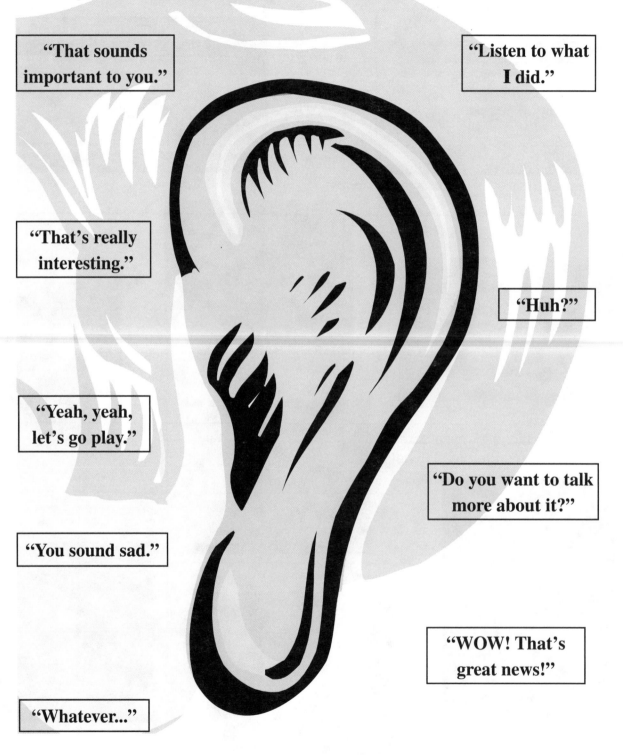

"That sounds important to you."

"Listen to what I did."

"That's really interesting."

"Huh?"

"Yeah, yeah, let's go play."

"Do you want to talk more about it?"

"You sound sad."

"WOW! That's great news!"

"Whatever..."

RATING YOUR EMPATHIC LISTENING

Directions: Look at the features of empathic listening listed below. Think about how well you do each one and rate yourself by putting a ✓ in one of the boxes under excellent, good, fair or poor. After you have rated yourself on each characteristic, put a ☆ by the one that you are best at and (circle) the one that you need to work on.

	Excellent	Good	Fair	Poor
I look at the speaker.				
I nod my head to show that I am interested.				
I lean forward to show that I am completely engaged in the conversation.				
I show an interested expression on my face.				
I stay on the speaker's subject until he/she is finished.				
I ask questions to make sure that I completely understand what the speaker is saying.				
I try to understand the speaker's feelings.				
I stop myself from daydreaming.				
I stop myself from interrupting.				
I truly care about what others have to say.				

EMPATHY & FEELING OTHERS' FEELINGS

OBJECTIVES:

At the end of this lesson students will be able to:

- Match their feelings with another person's feelings
- Relate to the feelings of others
- Use self-talk to motivate themselves to care

RATIONALE:

On a very basic level, emotional contagion (or the "catching" of feelings) is one of the precursors of empathy. All of us are aware of this phenomenon as we walk into a room where there is laughter or mourning. Our own mood is immediately changed to match that of those in the room. Students need to know that allowing themselves to be moved by others' emotions is not only a part of human nature, it is a trait that should be cultivated. This ability to share the feelings of others is what gives us a deep sense of belonging because we can "feel from the inside." Sharing the feelings of others is what truly makes empathy the social emotion.

MATERIALS:

Pencils and paper

SCRIPT:

After you have read someone else's feeling, it is important that you let yourself feel some of that feeling along with her/him. That doesn't mean that you will feel exactly the same as the other person, or to the same degree as that other person, but you will share some of the feeling with her/him. Think about when you play a game with someone. In order to play you must share a ball or a game board or something else related to the game. In order to have empathy with someone you must share the other person's feeling. The only exception to this would be the feeling of anger if it is directed towards you. Do not share this feeling or you will end up in an argument – and arguments are not empathy!

DISCUSSION QUESTIONS:

- Have you ever felt sad about something and you knew that someone felt sad with you? What was that experience like? How did it make you feel about the other person?
- When is it hard and when is it easy to feel other people's feelings? Does it matter if the person is someone you know? Does it matter what time of the day it is? Does it matter if you are in a particular mood yourself?
- What feelings are easy to feel with others and what feelings are more difficult to feel with others? For example, is it easier to feel sad with someone or proud with someone? Is it easier to feel embarrassed with someone or confused with someone?

EMPATHY & FEELING OTHERS' FEELINGS

ACTIVITIES:

Activity 1. *Breathing in Sync:* Ask students to break up into pairs. Instruct them to sit facing one another with their knees one inch apart (in other words, as close as possible without touching). Have one of the members of the pair close her/his eyes and think about something pleasant. Ask the other member of the pair to match the breathing rhythm of the person with his/her eyes closed. Do this for one minute and then have the students trade roles so that each student gets to match the breathing of the other.

Activity 2. *Mirroring:* Ask students to break up into pairs. Instruct them to sit facing one another with their knees one inch apart (in other words, as close as possible without touching). Have one member of the pair slowly make various feelings faces. Have the other person "mirror" those facial expressions – copying the exact look of the other's head, eyes, mouth, etc. Have the students trade roles so that each student gets to mirror the other.

Activity 3. *Imagine Empathy:* Invite students to get comfortable and to close their eyes. Guide them through a brief relaxation exercise and then through a guided imagery exercise where you ask them to imagine feeling another person's feelings. You can use the script/scenario below or create your own!

Get into a comfortable position and close your eyes. Now relax the top of your head. As the top of head gets relaxed, feel the relaxation melt down into your face and neck. Feel it move into your shoulders and chest. They are feeling so relaxed. In fact, the relaxed feeling is continuing to move down through your stomach and into your hips. Feel it melting down into the top of your legs; down through your knees and down through the calves of your legs. Relaxation has melted down completely through your legs and is now moving into your ankles, your heels and through your feet to the tips of your toes.

Now that you are completely and totally relaxed, I want you to imagine a boy in a wheelchair who is going to your school. Maybe you have seen him before and maybe you have not. He has wheeled himself over to a lunch table with some other students but the other students are ignoring him and continuing their conversation. Pretty soon the other students get up and go outside for recess. The boy in the wheelchair is left sitting alone at the table still eating his lunch. You look at him. His shoulders are slumped; his eyes are down; his mouth is also turned down; he eats very slowly. As you keep looking at him you start to feel sad. <pause> Then you realize that your own sad feelings are really part of the boy's sad feelings. You are sharing his sad feelings with him. You use your sad feelings to move you to do something. You walk over to him and ask him to join you and your friends at your table. As you help him pick up his lunch you can see that he is smiling and you are feeling happy too!

Now slowly open your eyes and tell yourself that you are a person that has empathy.

EMPATHY & FEELING OTHERS' FEELINGS

Activity 4. *Human Puppets:* Invite two (2) students to the front of the room. Ask one of the students to sit in a chair and briefly (in 1-2 sentences) tell the group about a recent experience. Direct the second student to stand behind the seated student and "talk for" her/him. The standing student will speak in first person as if s/he were the seated person, using the pronoun "I" instead of "He" or "She." S/he will describe the experience in more detail with a description of the thoughts and feelings that accompanied the experience.

Activity 5. *Letters to Characters:* Read a brief story about a character that faces some kind of obstacle(s). (Any story will do but a classic story that evokes a variety of feelings and is often very available in school libraries is *The Ugly Duckling.* Another recommended children's book is *Seemor's Flight to Freedom: A Book about Teasing and Anger Control* by K. Nightingale and N.L. Walter.) Instruct students to write a letter to one of the characters saying something that shows that they shared some of the character's feelings.

REPRODUCIBLE WORKSHEETS:

Worksheet 5.1, *Empathy and Self-Talk,* helps students to recognize how their internal dialogue contributes to the ability to allow themselves to feel others' feelings.

Worksheet 5.2, *Imagining What It Would Be Like,* asks students to imagine the feelings of a goldfish, a flower, a hospital and a pair of pants.

Worksheet 5.3, *If I Were in That Position,* is an activity that requires students to speculate what their own emotions would be if they were in situations experienced by others.

Worksheet 5.4, *Sharing Feelings,* invites students to think back to times when they shared a similar feeling with another person. They are asked to identify the person, the feeling and the situation.

Worksheet 5.5, *My Feeling Others' Feelings Journal,* is simply a diary that students may use to record the times that they are able to feel others' feelings. It is important for students to be able to document their successes at sharing others' feelings so that they can begin to see themselves as empathic persons.

EMPATHY & SELF-TALK

Directions: *What we tell ourselves is very important. It guides how we feel and act – including our abilities to calm our own feelings and to share others' feelings. We must tell ourselves how important it is for us to share others' feelings (i.e. "This news is quite sad. I don't know that I can do anything about it but I certainly feel sad for her."). Read each of the situations below. Change the negative self-talk to something that supports empathy.*

1) Larissa was tearful as she told you that even though she was selected for the lead part in the school play, she will not be able to do it because her parents won't let her. You say to yourself, "I can't do anything about it so I don't care." What would be something better to tell yourself that would allow you to share Larissa's feelings?

   _____

   _____

2) Abdul just fell off of the top of the highest slide in the park. He is laying on the ground screaming and there is blood on his shirt. You say to yourself, "This is too horrible, I have to leave." What would be something better to tell yourself that would allow you to share some of Abdul's feelings?

   _____

   _____

3) Cynthia is telling you about her trip to Mexico. It was her first time out of the country and she had a wonderful trip. She is telling you about the beach and the food and the animal life. You say to yourself, "This is so boring." What would be something better to tell yourself that would allow you to share some of Cynthia's feelings?

   _____

   _____

IMAGINING WHAT IT WOULD BE LIKE

Imagine what it would be like if you...

(1)......*were a goldfish*

What would make you happy? _____

What would make you sad? _____

What would surprise you? _____

(2)......*were a flower*

What would make you happy? _____

What would make you sad? _____

What would scare you? _____

(3)......*were a hospital*

What would make you happy? _____

What would make you sad? _____

What would make you angry? _____

(4)......*were a pair of pants*

What would make you happy? _____

What would make you sad? _____

What would embarrass you? _____

IF I WERE IN THAT POSITION

Directions: *Feeling others' feelings means that you connect with what it feels like to be in their situation. Complete the following sentences by writing in how you would feel in someone else's position and why.*

1. Peter had to stay in from recess because he was not finished with his math. If I were in Peter's position, I would feel _____ because

   _____.

2. Anna's best friend lied to her about going bowling on Saturday. If I were in Anna's position, I would feel _____ because _____

   _____.

3. Carlos is a great soccer player but he recently broke his leg and can't play for the entire spring season. If I were in Carlos's position, I would feel

   _____ because _____

   _____.

4. Antonio's shoes are falling apart and his parents can't afford to buy new ones because his father recently lost his job. If I were in Antonio's position, I

   would feel _____ because _____

   _____.

5. Heather just found out that her little brother, who was taken to the hospital after a car accident, is going to be okay. If I were in Heather's position, I would feel

   _____ because _____

   _____.

SHARING FEELINGS

Directions: *As humans we have the power to share feelings with others. Think of a time when you and someone else shared a feeling at the same time. Maybe you and a parent felt excited together when you watched a favorite sports team win; maybe both you and a friend felt disappointed when you couldn't do something together. On the pictures and spaces below write down the name of the person you shared a feeling with, the feeling that you shared, and the situation that caused the two of you to feel the same feeling.*

ME

My Friend,
_____

FEELING:

SITUATION:

_____

_____

_____

_____

ME

My Friend,
_____

FEELING:

SITUATION:

_____

_____

_____

_____

ME

My Friend,
_____

FEELING:

SITUATION:

_____

_____

_____

_____

MY FEELING OTHERS' FEELINGS JOURNAL

Directions: *Keep a journal each day of the times that you feel someone else's feelings. Write down the person's name, the feeling you shared with the person and what happened as a result of sharing feelings with that person.*

Monday

Friend: _____ Feeling: _____
Result: _____
_____

Tuesday

Friend: _____ Feeling: _____
Result: _____
_____

Wednesday

Friend: _____ Feeling: _____
Result: _____
_____

Thursday

Friend: _____ Feeling: _____
Result: _____
_____

Friday

Friend: _____ Feeling: _____
Result: _____
_____

Saturday

Friend: _____ Feeling: _____
Result: _____
_____

Sunday

Friend: _____ Feeling: _____
Result: _____
_____

EMPATHY & TEMPORARILY PUTTING YOUR OWN FEELINGS ASIDE

OBJECTIVES:

At the end of this lesson students will be able to:

- Recognize the need to regulate feelings (or temporarily put them aside) in order to practice empathy
- Identify strategies to regulate emotions
- Demonstrate the ability to think of others' thoughts and feelings

RATIONALE:

Empathy requires us to regulate our own emotions in the service of others' emotions. Research has shown that children who are overwhelmed with their own emotions are less empathic towards their peers (Klimes-Dougan & Kitner, 1990; Main & George, 1985). Therefore, before students can feel another's feelings they must be able to calm their own feelings. For example, if a student sees a peer fall off of a swing with a subsequent injury, the observing student may feel so overcome with fear and anxiety that s/he cannot offer assistance. Calming one's own distressed feelings is important in order to get attuned with the other person. This principle of setting one's own feelings aside temporarily in order to attend to another's feelings is included in Stephen Covey's, *The Seven Habits of Highly Effective People*. Covey states, "Seek first to understand, then to be understood." While this is an important principle for empathy development, it is also important to let students know that their feelings are not being ignored. They are simply being saved for later.

MATERIALS:

Several copies of Appendix D, four (4) large cardboard boxes, markers or crayons, paper and pencils

SCRIPT:

Can you hear someone else's whispers if you are screaming? <wait for response> Of course not! If you want to hear someone's whispers, you have to quiet your own voice so that you can hear the voice of the other person. That is like putting your own feelings aside temporarily so that you can feel the feelings of someone else. You have to "quiet" your feelings for a little while so that you can "hear" the feelings of someone else. That doesn't mean that your feelings don't count! On the contrary, your feelings are very important but sometimes it's necessary to put our feelings on hold and come back to them after we have matched someone else's feelings with her/him.

DISCUSSION QUESTIONS:

- Have you ever felt overwhelmed by your own feelings? What did you do?
- Have you ever had to put your feelings aside for something (i.e. not laugh during church or not get angry with your brother in front of your teacher)? How were you able to do that?
- Do you ever talk to yourself to get yourself to calm down or change your feelings? What do you tell yourself?
- Have you ever had to put your own feelings aside in order to share someone else's feelings? What made you do it?

EMPATHY & TEMPORARILY PUTTING YOUR OWN FEELINGS ASIDE

ACTIVITIES:

Activity 1. *Greek Chorus:* Explain to the group what a Greek chorus is (a company of actors who comment in unison on the thoughts or actions of the actors in a Greek play). Then, as a group, read the story in Appendix D with the facilitator reading the narration and the students reading the part of the "chorus."

Activity 2. *Feelings Pantomime:* Label 4 large boxes: 2 with the word, HAPPY, one with the word, JEALOUS, and one with the word, SAD. Ask two students to come to the front of the room for a psychodrama. Prior to the enactment of the psychodrama, ask one of the students (Student #1) to describe a real life wish/fantasy/dream to the group (i.e. getting a puppy, going to Disney World, being in the NBA, etc.). Then, for the psychodrama, announce to the group that the other student (Student #2) will be receiving Student #1's wish. Direct Student #2 to pick up one of the HAPPY boxes and carry it around in manner which depicts her/his happiness about the event. Then ask Student #1 to pick up the JEALOUS box and carry it around in manner which depicts her/his jealousy about the event (make sure that s/he moves away from Student #2 with the HAPPY box). Instruct Student #2 to look at Student #1's JEALOUS box and add the SAD on top of her/his HAPPY box. Then ask Student #1 to dramatize the difficulty in putting down the JEALOUSY box and picking up the HAPPY box. As s/he gets the HAPPY box securely lifted and secured, ask her/him to move closer to Student #1 while Student #2 puts down the SAD box. End the psychodrama with both students standing side-by-side, each holding a HAPPY box.

Activity 3. *Getting in Touch with Another's Feelings:* Ask students to sit in a circle; ask for a volunteer to come forward and sit in the middle of the circle. Instruct the student sitting in the middle (the volunteer) to share some kind of emotionally laden situation that has happened in her/his life. When the story is complete, direct the students to allow several seconds of silence as they "get in touch" with the feelings of the volunteer and allow themselves to feel the feeling themselves. Discuss how easy/difficult it was to lay aside one's own thoughts and feelings about the situation and to be present with the person in the center. Repeat the exercise so that everyone who would like to gets an opportunity to be in the center of the circle.

Activity 4. *How Well Do I Know Others?:* Give each student a piece of paper and a pencil. Invite one of the students to the front of the room. Ask the remaining students to think about the student in the front of the room (not themselves). Explain that you will read a question and the students are to guess from the four choices how they think the student in the front of the room will respond. Instruct the students to write down the letter of the choice that they select. After everyone has written down the letter of their response choice, ask the student in the front of the room what the correct answer is. See how many correct responses there are. Repeat this until everyone has had several chances to be the one in the front of the class. Potential questions are limitless with this activity. Some suggestions for questions and answers are:

EMPATHY & TEMPORARILY PUTTING YOUR OWN FEELINGS ASIDE

QUESTION: *What makes you feel most angry?*
CHOICES: *a) When kids make fun of you*
   b) When your teacher blames you for something you didn't do
   c) When your brother or sister uses your stuff without asking
   d) When someone pushes you out of line

QUESTION: *What makes you feel happiest?*
CHOICES: *a) Friends*
   b) Good grades
   c) Money
   d) Being good at sports

QUESTION: *What makes you feel most nervous?*
CHOICES: *a) Scary movies*
   b) High places
   c) Oral book reports
   d) Your dad's anger

QUESTION: *If you could have one wish come true, what would it be?*
CHOICES: *a) To live forever*
   b) To have lots of money
   c) To be famous
   d) To be the smartest person in the world

QUESTION: *How would you feel if a group of kids wouldn't let you play with them?*
CHOICES: *a) Angry*
   b) Sad
   c) Disappointed
   d) Embarrassed

QUESTION: *How would you feel if you found out you were moving to another state?*
CHOICES: *a) Excited*
   b) Sad
   c) Anxious
   d) Mixed

QUESTION: *If you could go to any of these countries, which would you go to?*
CHOICES: *a) South Africa*
   b) China
   c) Canada
   d) Antarctica

EMPATHY & TEMPORARILY PUTTING YOUR OWN FEELINGS ASIDE

REPRODUCIBLE WORKSHEETS:

Worksheet 6.1, *Calming My Feelings,* uses a cognitive approach to address two (2) different scenarios where the student would feel one way and a peer would feel another way. In both cases the student is asked to lay her/his own feelings aside in order to attend to the feelings of the friend.

Worksheet 6.2, *Controlling My Feelings,* asks students to interpret a quotation from Aristotle that states, "I count him braver who overcomes his desires than him who conquers his enemies, for the hardest victory is the victory over self" and then to identify the ways in which they sooth themselves when they are feeling worried, angry or disappointed.

Worksheet 6.3, *Empathy Tic-Tac-Toe,* asks students to differentiate behaviors that show empathy and behaviors that show concern for the self. This is in a traditional tic-tac-toe format where X's and Os are used in order to find lines of similar symbols. The worksheet has two (2) tic-tac-toes after all of the spaces have been marked.

Worksheet 6.4, *Thinking of Others,* instructs students to again determine behaviors which show the setting aside of one's own feelings in the service of someone else. Students are asked to color those behaviors which show empathy with their favorite color and to color the selfish behaviors BLACK.

Worksheet 6.5, *Empathy for Adversaries,* presents the idea that we can still allow ourselves to feel empathy with those who we do not like. This may be the ultimate in setting your own feelings aside in order to attend to the feelings of another! Students are asked to think of two (2) people that they do not like but are instructed not to say their names out loud. As they think about these children, they are to write down one good quality or ability for each one of them and then what things they have in common with those children.

CALMING MY FEELINGS

DIRECTIONS: Read the scenarios below and fill in the blanks.

(1) You and your friend, Caitlin, both tried out for the lead part in the school play. Caitlin was selected. How do you feel?_____ How does she feel? _____ She is hopping up and down and running around telling everyone. When she approaches you she asks why you aren't happy for her. What can you tell yourself so that you can put your own feelings aside for awhile in order to share her happiness? _____

_____What do you

say to Caitlin now? _____

(2) Your parents just told you that you could get a new puppy. They plan to take you to pick it out this evening. How do you feel? _____ Two minutes later your best friend calls and says his grandfather just had a heart attack and went into the hospital. How does he feel? _____ What can you tell yourself so that you can put your own feelings aside for awhile in order to share his distress?

_____

_____ What do you say to your friend now?

_____

CONTROLLING MY FEELINGS

A famous philosopher, Aristotle said, "I count him braver who overcomes his desires than him who conquers his enemies, for the hardest victory is the victory over self." What do you think that this means?

_____

_____

_____

Write down two (2) ways that you calm yourself when you are feeling worried.

(1)

(2)

Write down two (2) ways that you calm yourself when you are feeling angry.

(1)

(2)

Write down two (2) ways that you calm yourself when you are feeling disappointed.

(1)

(2)

EMPATHY TIC-TAC-TOE

DIRECTIONS: *Put an O over the statements that describe behaviors that show empathy and put an X over the statements that only show concern for yourself. How many tic-tac-toes do you get?*

Congratulating your friend on winning the class spelling bee	**Waiting for a friend to get her coat on before going outside to recess**	**Saying, "Hurry-up" to someone who is a slow reader**
Laughing at someone's new haircut	**Playing what your friend wants to play even if it's not your favorite thing to do**	**Complaining about dinner at your friend's house**
Grabbing the first piece of cake at a birthday party	**Saying, "Nice try" to a teammate who failed to make a goal in soccer**	**Sending a" Get Well" card to someone who has been sick for awhile**

THINKING OF OTHERS

DIRECTIONS: *Which of the following behaviors shows that you are putting your own feelings aside so that you can show empathy for someone else? Color these in your favorite color. Color the ones that show selfishness rather than empathy* **BLACK**.

Even though you are "starving," you let someone go ahead of you in the lunch line because his class has already gone through.

You help a friend with her homework because she asked you to - even though you think it's easy.

You listen to your friend's problem even though your other friends want you to come outside and play.

You take the biggest piece of cake because you are really hungry.

Your parents are sleeping late on Saturday morning but your sister is being a brat so you go tell on her.

You can see that your teacher is not feeling well but you ask her to stay after class to help you with math.

Your brother is late for his game but he has to clean the hamster cage. You think, "Too bad!"

Your sister's computer games got stolen. You loan her some of your favorites.

You help a bully pick up the books that he dropped in the middle of the hallway.

EMPATHY FOR ADVERSARIES

DIRECTIONS: *Think of 2 people that you do not like.* **DO NOT** *say their names out loud. Simply think about them. Decide who you want to be Person #1 and who you want to be Person #2. Then answer the following questions regarding each person:*

PERSON #1

(1)   What is one good quality or ability you have noticed about this person?

_____

_____

(2)   Name 3 things you have in common with this person. If you have trouble thinking of something, go find out more about this person by asking her/his friends or relatives.

_____

_____

_____

PERSON #2

(3)   What is one good quality or ability you have noticed about this person?

_____

_____

(4)   Name 3 things you have in common with this person. If you have trouble thinking of something, go find out more about this person by asking her/his friends or relatives.

_____

_____

_____

EMPATHY & MAKING SUPPORTIVE STATEMENTS

OBJECTIVES:

At the end of this lesson students will be able to:

- Understand the importance of making supportive statements
- Verbally show an interest in others
- Identify appropriate expressions of concern for various situations
- Demonstrate the use of supportive statements

RATIONALE:

As discussed in the introduction, empathy not only includes perspective-taking and emotional congruence, it involves a behavioral response. Often times this behavioral response is in the form of supportive communication. Supportive communication can come early in an interaction such as showing an interest in someone or it can come later when one is responding to another's situation. Communication is important to relationships and important to empathy expression and the exchange of feelings.

MATERIALS:

At least two (2) puppets, a copy of Appendix E, scissors, tape, tissues, a TV, a video or DVD (optional), paper, pencils and crayons/markers

SCRIPT:

When good things happen to people it's easy to know what to say. We tell them things like "Congratulations" or "You are so lucky" or "I'm really happy for you." It's not so easy to know what to say when bad things happen to people. It makes us feel uncomfortable. Sometimes it's good to say something hopeful and encouraging, and other times its better to say something that shows you are aware of the person's sad feelings. One "Rule of Thumb" is:

When the bad situation is something that is not fixable (i.e. a pet dies) it is better to simply let the person know that you are sorry to hear the news and are sharing their sad feelings with them. If it is a situation that can possibly be changed (i.e. a sweater is lost) it might be okay to say something encouraging.

DISCUSSION QUESTIONS:

- Have you ever felt like you didn't know what to say to someone? What did you do?
- Have you ever used your words to cheer someone up who was feeling sad? Has anyone ever used their words to cheer you up when you were feeling sad? What was that experience like for you?
- How do you think others feel when you say supportive things to them? Do you think that this is important in a relationship?
- How do you show an interest in others? How does it feel when others show an interest in you?

EMPATHY & MAKING SUPPORTIVE STATEMENTS

ACTIVITIES:

Activity 1. *Empathy Puppet Show:* Ask two (2) students to come to the front of the room. Give them each a puppet and ask them to portray the following scenario. One of the puppets has tried out for a premier soccer team but did not make the team and is now very disappointed and sad. The other puppet is asking what is the matter and is making an empathic statement after s/he finds out what the situation is. Have the students repeat the puppet show three (3) times – each time using a different response (listed below). Ask the audience to decide which response they think is the best one.

- "I guess you'll just have to practice harder for next year."
- "Jermaine made the team!"
- "I'm really sorry that you didn't make it."

Now ask two (2) different students to come to the front of the room. Again, give them each a puppet and ask them to portray the following scenario. One of the puppets has just found out that his family dog of twelve (12) years has died. He chokes up whenever he talks about it. The other puppet just found out what happened from another friend and is making an empathic statement. Again, have the students repeat this scenario three (3) times –each time using a different response (listed below). Ask the audience to decide which response they think is the best one.

- "How about if I buy you a new dog?"
- "I'm so sorry to hear about your dog. Is there anything I can do?"
- "Hey, do you want to go play some basketball?"

Activity 2. *Is It Support or Is It Trash?:* Using the materials in Appendix E, cut out the supportive and unsupportive statements. Then hang the pictures of Trash and Supportive on opposite walls of the room. Mix up the supportive and unsupportive statements and distribute them among the students. Depending on their content, have students tape their statements to either the picture of Trash (for unsupportive statements) and or the picture of Supportive (for supportive statements). After all of the statements are taped to the two (2) sheets, read the statements on each sheet out loud.

Activity 3. *Empathy Referee:* Hand each student 10 tissues and explain that these are to be used as "penalty flags." Explain that as they view a segment from a cartoon or TV show (this can be a show that is on TV at the time of the group or a video/DVD), they are to throw down one tissue as a "penalty flag" for each unsupportive statement that is made. When supportive statements are made they are to put both of their arms in the air (a referee's gesture for a successful touchdown).

Activity 4. *Measuring Supportive Statements:* Have students draw a large thermometer on a piece of paper. Explain that this thermometer represents the different "temperatures" of liking something. (The bottom of the thermometer represents neutral feelings and the top of the thermometer represents extremely positive feelings.) Tell the students that you will be reading six (6) numbers with situations and supportive/empathic statements. They will write the number of the statement somewhere on the thermometer which represents the level of how much they would like hearing the statement. Supportive/empathic statements:

EMPATHY & MAKING SUPPORTIVE STATEMENTS

1. Your swimming teacher has asked you to swim the length of the pool. Someone says, "I bet you can do it."

2. You tried to make a basket and missed. Someone says, "Good try!"

3. You just dropped a pile of papers on the floor in the hallway at school. Someone asks, "Can I help?"

4. Someone accidentally bumps you in the hall and says, "I'm sorry."

5. You tell the person sitting next to you that your grandparents are moving away and the person says, "Man, that's really tough."

6. You just found out that you won a $50 gift certificate for a poster contest. Someone says, "Congratulations!"

Activity 5. *Showing Interest in Another:* Invite two (2) students to the front of the room to role-play how one would show an interest in a new student. Ask one of the students to play the new student (Student A) and the other to play the student that has been at the school for several years (Student B). Instruct the Student B to introduce her/himself to Student A and to show an interest in Student A by asking questions about the student. Make sure that questions don't get asked one right after another like an interrogation. Instruct the Student B to ask open-ended questions (i.e. "What" and "How" questions) and to make comments between questions that show an interest (i.e. "Hmmmm," "Really?!" "That sounds interesting," etc.).

REPRODUCIBLE WORKSHEETS:

Worksheet 7.1, *Choosing Empathic Statements,* asks students to consider particular scenarios and, using a multiple choice format, to select the best empathic response to each situation.

Worksheet 7.2, *What is Encouragement?,* invites students to examine several situations where children are faced with challenges and to select an encouraging statement from two (2) pictured statements.

Worksheet 7.3, *Wrong Time and Right Time,* challenges students to think about the right time and wrong time to make certain remarks by asking them to identify when a particular verbalization is appropriate or inappropriate.

Worksheet 7.4, *Making My Own Empathic Statements,* instructs students to write down their own empathic verbal responses to statements that others might make.

Worksheet 7.5, *Showing an Interest in Others,* asks students to look at pictures of children involved in various activities and to identify questions that show an interest in the other person's activities.

CHOOSING EMPATHIC STATEMENTS

DIRECTIONS: *Read each of the following situations and the responses that are listed under them. Put a checkmark in front of the response that best shows empathy.*

1. Your mother's best friend is in the hospital with a serious illness and your mother is quite worried about her.

   ❑ You ask if you can go to the hospital to see the friend.

   ❑ You ask your mother what is for dinner to distract her from her worry.

   ❑ You offer to do some extra chores so that your mother can have time to go to the hospital to see her friend.

   ❑ You tell your mother that it is silly to be so worried.

2. Your best friend is really excited because he just got a really cool computer game. It was a game that you had wanted.

   ❑ You ask if you can borrow it.

   ❑ You feel jealous so you change the subject and won't talk about it.

   ❑ You go home and beg your parent to buy you one.

   ❑ You say, "That's great" and tell him that he deserves getting such a cool game.

3. A new student in your school is lost and can't find the office. He looks really scared and confused.

   ❑ You tell your friends that the new kid is lost.

   ❑ You go up to him and say, "Its tough being new kid. Can I help you find your class?"

   ❑ You go on to your own class assuming that he'll figure it out.

   ❑ You go up to him and say, "Its tough finding your way around here. Good luck finding your class!"

4. Your friend is getting ready to go into the play-offs with her soccer team and she is pretty nervous.

   ❑ You go hang out with another friend who is in a better mood.

   ❑ You say, "Its just soccer! Don't worry about it!"

   ❑ You tell her you understand how she feels because you were really nervous, too, before your big game last year.

   ❑ You tell her to "Chill out."

WHAT IS ENCOURAGEMENT?

DIRECTIONS: *Read the students' situations on the left. Then circle the student on the right who is saying something encouraging to the student on the left.*

WRONG TIME AND RIGHT TIME

DIRECTIONS: *Being empathic also means knowing when it is the right time to say something and when it is the wrong time to say something. Read and answer the questions below.*

1. When is it the wrong time to laugh at someone? _____

_____

1a. When is the right time to laugh at someone? _____

_____

2. When is it the wrong time to say, "You're silly?" _____

_____

2a. When is the right time to say, "You're silly?" _____

_____

3. When is it the wrong time to yell at someone? _____

_____

3a. When is the right time to yell at someone? _____

_____

4. When is it the wrong time to give a compliment? _____

_____

4a. When is the right time to give a compliment? _____

_____

MAKING MY OWN EMPATHIC STATEMENTS

DIRECTIONS: *Read the situations below and then use the speech bubbles to write down something empathic that you could say.*

A classmate looks sad and says, "No one likes me."

_____
_____
_____

A friend hates to read out loud because he stutters.

_____
_____
_____

Your sister's boyfriend just broke up with her.

_____
_____
_____

SHOWING AN INTEREST IN OTHERS

DIRECTIONS: *Look at the pictures below. If you were going to strike up a conversation with each of the children pictured, what would you say or ask to show that you were interested in them and the things that they do?*

EMPATHY AND DOING SUPPORTIVE THINGS

OBJECTIVES:

At the end of this lesson students will be able to:

- Understand the importance of translating empathic feelings into empathic behaviors
- Identify several supportive/empathic behaviors
- Understand the effects of actions on others

RATIONALE:

Research shows that there is a strong relationship between empathy and prosocial behaviors (e.g. Portner, 1997; Strayer & Roberts, 1989). People who are able to feel another's feelings and cognitively put themselves "in the others' shoes" are more likely to behave in ways that are compassionate and helpful. However, not all feelings lead to action so it is important to teach students to, not only allow themselves to share the feelings of others, but to allow those shared feelings to produce caring and cooperative behaviors.

In addition, it is important for students to understand the impact that their behaviors have on others' feelings. When one exhibits caring behaviors, others feel nurtured, supported and close. When one exhibits insensitive or callous behaviors, others feel neglected, angry and distant.

MATERIALS:

Paper, pencils, hat or small box, *Chicken Soup for the Kid's Soul: 101 Stories of Courage, Hope and Laughter,* construction paper, white paper, stapler with staples, crayons or markers, scissors and glue

SCRIPT:

When you have empathy and feel another person's feelings it usually causes you to want to do something. For example, if I share someone's sad feelings I may want to put my arm around the person or get her/him a tissue; if I share someone's embarrassed feelings I may want to help her/him get out of the embarrassing situation. Empathy pushes us towards action – action that is helpful, cooperative and caring. These helpful, cooperative and caring behaviors in turn give us positive feelings about ourselves and a positive reputation among others. In fact, studies have shown that the more someone does nice things, the more other kids like her/him!

DISCUSSION QUESTIONS:

- How do our actions affect other people?
- What are caring behaviors?
- When was a time that you did something that was caring, helpful or supportive? How did that feel to you? How did the other person feel?
- When is it easy to do things that are caring, helpful or supportive? When is it hard?
- What are "random acts of kindness?"

EMPATHY AND DOING SUPPORTIVE THINGS

ACTIVITIES:

Activity 1. *Secret Angels:* Ask students to write their names on slips of paper. Mix up these slips of paper in a hat or box and then ask each child to select a name. Do not let anyone share the name that they have drawn and do not let anyone select their own name. Then explain to the students that they are to be the "Secret Angel" for the person whose name they have drawn. "Secret Angel" activities are essentially random acts of kindness. You can keep the "Secret Angel" activities going for an hour or for a day or for a week.

Activity 2. *Stories of Empathy:* Select and read a story of empathy and kind behavior from *Chicken Soup for the Kid's Soul: 101 Stories of Courage, Hope and Laughter* by Jack Canfield, Mark Victor Hansen, Patty Hansen & Irene Dunlap or from *Monday Morning Messages* by Tom Carr (or any other inspirational, empathic stories).

Activity 3. *Random Acts of Kindness:* Declare a Random Acts of Kindness week. Brainstorm some of the acts of kindness that students could do and then encourage them to actually do them over the week. At the end of the seven (7) days discuss how it felt to do nice things for no specific reason. Discuss the impact of their acts of kindness on the recipients of the kindness. For information on activities, newsletters, quotations, and other helpful information go to http://www.actsofkindness.org.

Activity 4. *Name that Helping Activity:* Ask students to name ways that they can help others at home and at school. Role-play some of these scenarios. Ideas might include helping someone with schoolwork, helping someone with chores, helping someone find their way, helping someone open a door, helping someone look for something, etc. Talk about how it feels to help and to be helped.

Activity 5. *A Sharing Book:* Have students create a My Sharing Book. Using construction paper for the covers, white paper for the pages, and staples to hold the "book" together, instruct students to draw pictures of times when they have shared things. Have students show their books to the group. Ask students what kinds of people do the things that are pictured in their books (getting them to identify themselves as kind, generous or empathic people).

Activity 6. *Let's Go Help:* Arrange for the students to do a volunteer project for a needy group in your community. Examples might include collecting nonperishable items for a food bank, collecting toys for a children's wing in a hospital, helping at an animal shelter, singing at a nursing home, etc.

EMPATHY AND DOING SUPPORTIVE THINGS

REPRODUCIBLE WORKSHEETS:

Worksheet 8.1, *Choosing Empathic Behaviors,* asks students to consider particular scenarios and, using a multiple choice format, to select the best empathic behavior for each situation.

Worksheet 8.2, *Lending a Helping Hand,* invites students to recognize times when they have been helpful and to identify the feelings associated with these behaviors.

Worksheet 8.3, *Rating My Empathic Behaviors,* instructs students to read over a list of empathic behaviors and to color in stars next to each behavior to rate how well they think they perform each one.

Worksheet 8.4, *Acts of Empathy Dice,* should be cut out and glued so that it makes into a square box (a "dice") with the six (6) written behaviors showing on the outside. Students can use this to play in group. It asks them to clean up something in the room, to compliment the person on their left, to write a thank-you note to the custodian, to give a person a pat on the back, ask the person who is less known to play at recess, and to do something requested for the person on the right.

Worksheet 8.5, *Identifying Empathic Behaviors,* asks students to examine pictures of empathic behaviors and then to identify what the person is doing that shows empathy. The pictures include helping someone in a wheelchair, sharing a drink with someone who doesn't have one, helping someone carry something heavy, comforting someone with a gentle touch and helping someone read.

CHOOSING EMPATHIC BEHAVIORS

DIRECTIONS: *Read each of the following situations and the responses. Circle the response that best shows empathy.*

(1) Your friend keeps getting teased and bullied on the playground.

    (a) You stay away so that you do not get teased.

    (b) You join in with the teasing so you'll look cool.

    (c) You stick up for your friend.

    (d) You find another friend.

(2) Your friend can't find her social studies homework.

    (a) You compliment her new haircut.

    (b) You walk away so she can find it herself.

    (c) You laugh at her.

    (d) You help her look for it.

(3) Your mother comes home from work stressed out from a hard day.

    (a) You invite some friends over.

    (b) You set the table and help her get dinner ready.

    (c) You whine about her being grumpy.

    (d) You turn up the TV.

(4) Your sister has to clean up a huge mess in her room that her friends left.

    (a) You walk away.

    (b) You call a friend and laugh about it.

    (c) You shut the door so you don't have to look at it.

    (d) You help her pick up her room.

(5) Your friend is in the hospital having surgery.

    (a) You think, "Thank goodness it's not me!"

    (b) You invite your other friends over for a sleepover.

    (c) You send him a Get Well card with a joke book.

    (d) You try not to think about it.

LENDING A HELPING HAND

DIRECTIONS: *There are many ways that people show empathy by lending a helping hand. What are some of the ways that you have helped someone? Name at least 3 times when you have lent a helping hand.*

#1. _____

_____

#2. _____

_____

#3. _____

_____

How did you feel after each of these times of lending a helping hand?

#1. _____

#2. _____

#3. _____

What do you think this says about you as a person?

_____

_____

_____

RATING MY EMPATHIC BEHAVIOR

DIRECTIONS: *There are lots of ways that you can show you care with empathic behaviors. Listed below are several of these behaviors. Rate your habit of doing each one by coloring in the stars. Coloring in all 5 stars means that you are outstanding at doing this empathic behavior; 4 stars means you are good at it; 3 stars means you are fair at it; 2 stars means you are not so good at it and 1 star means you could really use some work on this behavior!*

Sharing your things with others ☆☆☆☆☆

Giving birthday gifts ☆☆☆☆☆

Complimenting others ☆☆☆☆☆

Remembering people's names ☆☆☆☆☆

Including people who get left out ☆☆☆☆☆

Sending cards to cheer others up ☆☆☆☆☆

Helping people ☆☆☆☆☆

Waiting for people ☆☆☆☆☆

Giving people hugs ☆☆☆☆☆

Comforting people who are crying ☆☆☆☆☆

ACTS OF EMPATHY DICE

DIRECTIONS: *Cut out the figure below. Then cut on the dotted lines. Fold on the solid lines and glue or tape the blank portions, making sure that they go into the inside of the dice. Roll the dice and do the thing that is written on the side facing up. Play with your friends!*

Give the person on your left a compliment.	**Write a thank you note to the custodian.**	**Clean up something in this room.**
	Invite the person you least know in this group to play with you at recess.	
	Ask the person on your right what she / he would like you to do for her / him. Do it.	
	Give the person across from you a pat on the back.	

IDENTIFYING EMPATHIC BEHAVIORS

DIRECTIONS: Look at the pictures below. Each of them shows an empathic behavior. In the spaces below each picture, write what the person is doing that shows empathy.

_____

_____

_____

_____

_____

_____

_____

_____

_____

EMPATHY & MAKING / KEEPING FRIENDS

OBJECTIVES:

At the end of this lesson students will be able to:

- State the "Golden Rule" and describe what it means
- Describe cooperation
- Recognize what makes others feel liked or special
- Identify what people want in a friend

RATIONALE:

Students who have difficulty reading and feeling others' feelings may also have difficulty making and keeping friends. Research shows that children's relationships with their friends support cooperation and reciprocity (Hartup & Laursen, 1992). Children view friends as people who understand them. Empathy conveys this understanding and reciprocity.

MATERIALS:

Paper, crayons/markers, pencils, 7-piece preschool puzzles, balloons, index cards and copies of Appendix F

SCRIPT:

Everyone likes to have friends. Friends are great for several reasons: they play with you; they help you celebrate special occasions; they listen to your problems; they keep you from feeling lonely; and they stick up for you. Friends can sometimes understand you better because they are the same age. But to have a friend you must be a friend. And to be a true friend you must have empathy.

Being a true friend means that you care about and share your friend's feelings. You are able to understand your friend because you can see the world through their eyes. You trust one another because you accept one another's feelings and points of view. You often feel closest to a friend when you have shared a sad time together or when you have needed each other for support.

DISCUSSION QUESTIONS:

- Why is it important to have friends? What are friends good for?
- What are some ways that you can make friends? What are some ways that you can keep friends after you make them?
- What do people look for in a friend?
- What are some ways that you can make friends feel special?

EMPATHY & MAKING / KEEPING FRIENDS

ACTIVITIES:

Activity 1. *Making A Friend Feel Special:* Give students a piece of paper and ask them to draw and color a fairly large picture of a friend who is not among the group in the room (thereby avoiding the possibility of someone getting left out). Then ask students to write something on the torso of the picture that they think they could do to make this person feel special. Then direct students to cut out the drawings of their friends. Cut-out drawings can be used to decorate a Friendship Bulletin Board.

Activity 2. *Cooperation:* Ask students to break up into groups of three (3). Discuss the skills of cooperation – i.e. listening, sharing, no put-downs, working together equally, etc. Then give each group a 7-piece preschool puzzle turned upside down on the table so that the picture cannot be seen. Ask the small groups to work together to put the puzzle together (not looking at the picture underneath!) stressing that the groups work cooperatively. When the puzzles are complete ask group members to give each other feedback regarding their cooperation skills and to give each other specific compliments.

Activity 3. *Being Mindful of Another:* Divide students into pairs so that everyone has a partner. Ask each pair to sit in chairs and to face one another (distance between partners can be modified based on age and/or gross motor skill abilities). Hand each pair a blown-up balloon and ask students to bat the balloon back and forth between themselves as many times as they can without getting out of their seats. See which pair can keep the balloon in the air the longest. Afterwards discuss what skills were needed to be successful. Pay particular attention to the skills that address being mindful of the other person.

Activity 4. *Friendship Report Card:* Create small groups of 3 - 4 students. Ask groups to come up with a Friendship Report Card. Have them list 5 - 10 friendship skills that would be on this "grade card." Then ask individuals to "grade" themselves using this grade card. Remind them to be honest with themselves!

Activity 5. *Giving Compliments:* Ask students to sit in a circle. Explain that a compliment is an expression of appreciation, value, affection, or admiration; it is saying something to another person that lets her/him know something that you like about her/him. Ask students to give the student on their right some kind of compliment. Go around the entire circle so that everyone has both given and received a compliment. If students need prompts for thinking of compliments, ask them to consider what behaviors/skills/personality qualities they like about the person. Students may also use copies of Appendix F for ideas for compliments.

Activity 6. *Building Trust:* Discuss with the group the importance of trust in a relationship. Explain that trusting another person means that you can rely on, count on, be sure about, have faith in him/her. Then divide students into pairs so that everyone has a partner. Give each pair of students a piece of paper and a pencil and ask them to write the letters in the word trust going down the page. Have pairs brainstorm and write down phrases that describe trust using each letter in the word to begin a phrase. For example:

EMPATHY & MAKING / KEEPING FRIENDS

- **T** reating each other kindly
- **R** especting each other
- **U** nderstanding each other
- **S** ticking up for one another
- **T** aking time to be together

REPRODUCIBLE WORKSHEETS:

Worksheet 9.1, *Friendly Attitude,* directs students to follow specific directions in order to find a word that describes an attitude that assists in making and keeping friends. FYI: the hidden word is caring.

Worksheet 9.2, *What do People Want from a Friend?,* asks students to list five (5) characteristics they think others are looking for in a friend. It then instructs them to identify the two (2) characteristics that they believe are the most important. Finally, it directs them to "grade" themselves on all five (5) of the characteristics.

Worksheet 9.3, *Really Knowing a Friend,* explains to students how important it is to know a person in order to call her/him a friend. It invites them to examine (and consequently, be sensitive to!) varying parts of a friend's life. The four (4) parts that they are to explore include the Brothers & sisters, Favorite foods, Hobbies and Favorite subject in school.

Worksheet 9.4, *Making Others Feel Special,* describes how empathy inspires us to learn what others like and dislike. It invites students to write down the names of five (5) people they know and to identify things that make each one of them feel special.

Worksheet 9.5, *The Golden Rule,* emphasizes the importance of treating others the way we would like to be treated. It asks students to identify how they would like to be treated and how they would not like to be treated.

FRIENDLY ATTITUDE

DIRECTIONS: *What kind of attitude does it take to have good friends? Follow the directions below. Then use the leftover letters to find the answer.*

- Cross off all the P's and Q's
- Cross off all the vowels in Column 4
- Cross off all the letters in Row C that come after R in the alphabet
- Cross off all the letters in Column 2 that come before F in the alphabet
- Cross off all the consonants in Row D
- Cross off all the T's and B's

	1	2	3	4	5	6
A	C	E	P	A	Q	T
B	B	Q	A	O	T	P
C	S	D	W	P	R	V
D	Q	Z	P	E	X	I
E	B	C	Q	N	T	Q
F	Q	G	T	P	B	P

____ ____ ____ ____ ____ ____ **!!**

WHAT DO PEOPLE WANT FROM A FRIEND?

DIRECTIONS: *All of us need and enjoy friendships. Think about kids your age and the friendships that they have. What do you think they want from their friends? Make a list of the qualities/behaviors that you think kids your age are looking for in a friend (i.e. honesty). After you have brainstormed a list of at least 5 qualities/behaviors that you think kids are looking for in a friend, put stars by the 2 qualities/behaviors that you think are most important.*

FRIENDSHIP BEHAVIORS	"GRADE"
_____	_____
_____	_____
_____	_____
_____	_____
_____	_____

*Now give yourself a "grade" on each of these qualities/behaviors. How well do **YOU** show these qualities?*

A = Excellent   B = Good   C = Average   D = Poor

REALLY KNOWING A FRIEND

An important part of making and keeping friends is to really know the other person. That helps us to understand and better consider her/his needs. How well do you know your friend?

DIRECTIONS: *Think of a friend. Then, inside the sections of the circle below, write down as many things as you can think of for each area of your friend's life.*

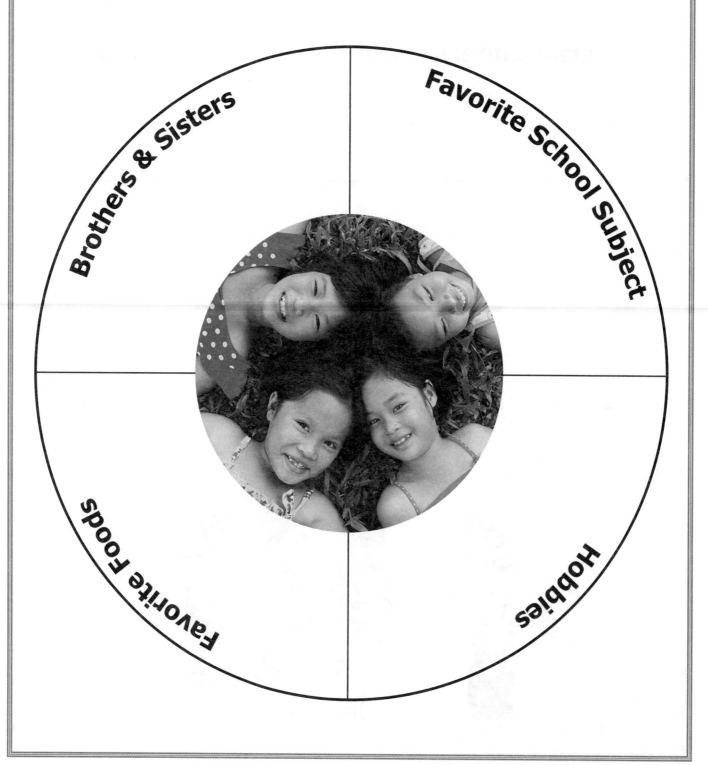

Brothers & Sisters

Favorite School Subject

Favorite Foods

Hobbies

MAKING OTHERS FEEL SPECIAL

Empathy leads us into learning what others like and dislike. In fact, one of the best ways to make and keep friends is to make others feel special. Different people feel special for different reasons. Some people like to be listened to; some people like to receive notes; some people like to be invited places; etc.

DIRECTIONS: *Write down the names of 5 people that you know. Then write down what you think makes them feel special.*

FRIEND	What Makes Her / Him Feel Special
#1	
#2	
#3	
#4	
#5	

THE GOLDEN RULE
"TREAT OTHERS THE WAY YOU WANT TO BE TREATED."

Almost every religion has a version of the Golden Rule. That is because it is an important truth about empathy and our fellow human beings.

DIRECTIONS: *Think about how you would like to be treated. Then read the statements below. If you would like to be treated in the way that is described, circle the thumbs up sign; if you would not like to be treated in the way that is described, circle the thumbs down sign.*

Would you like it if.......

......someone laughed at your new shoes?

......someone paid attention to your oral book report?

......someone helped you pick up the books your dropped?

......someone didn't apologize after bumping into you?

......someone invited you to their birthday party?

......someone said you couldn't play with their group?

......someone made fun of the way you throw a ball?

......someone let you choose what to play?

EMPATHY AND CONFLICT RESOLUTION

OBJECTIVES:

At the end of this lesson students will be able to:

- Recognize that empathy is an important element in conflict resolution
- Understand the concept of "win-win"
- Identify a variety of conflict resolution strategies

RATIONALE:

Effective conflict resolution always involves empathy and being able to see the situation from the other person's point of view. The probability of finding a mutually agreeable solution is greatly increased when both parties seek to understand the other person's thoughts, feelings and actions. Seeking to understand the one we differ from may be the most difficult time to practice empathy but doing so stimulates creative problem-solving and creates win-win solutions.

MATERIALS:

Paper, pencils, poster boards, crayons or markers, scissors and glue

SCRIPT:

A conflict is when two or more people disagree with each other or have an argument. They might have a difference of opinion or one might not like something that the other person did. Conflicts can make people feel angry, hurt, sad, put down, powerless and even scared. Conflict resolution is when people try to resolve or settle their disagreement. Empathy really comes in handy when you are trying to resolve your conflicts because understanding the other person's point of view can help you find solutions that are good for both of you! When you are able to find solutions that are good for both people, this is called a "win-win" solution rather than a "win-lose" solution. It is important to have empathy as you try to find "win-win" solutions!

DISCUSSION QUESTIONS:

- Have you ever had a disagreement with someone? Were you able to see the situation from the other person's point of view? Were you able to resolve it? How?
- What feelings do you have when you have a conflict with someone?
  What feelings does the other person have when they have a conflict with you?
- What does it mean to compromise?
- What do you think it means to agree to disagree?
- What are the benefits of being good at conflict resolution?

EMPATHY AND CONFLICT RESOLUTION

ACTIVITIES:

Activity 1. *Rules for Fair Fighting:* Put students in small groups of 3-4. Have them brainstorm a list of "rules" for good conflict resolution (i.e. no name calling, take turns talking, try to understand the other's feelings, etc.). Ask one of the students to take notes for the group and then ask each group to share their "rules."

Activity 2. *Empathy in Conflict Role-Play:* Ask two (2) students at a time to role-play various conflicts. Stop the conflict after a few minutes and ask each student how they think the other person feels and what they think the other person wants. Ask the students to come up with a "win-win" solution. Situations to role-play might include some of the following:

- Both students want to play with the same ball. One wants to use it with her/his friends to play four-square and the other one wants to use it with her/his friends to play dodgeball.
- One student confronts another student rather aggressively because s/he told something that was supposed to be a secret.
- Both students are building something together but one of them starts to take over and the other student is feeling left out and frustrated.
- One student is over at another student's house. The mother says that she will take them out to lunch. One wants to go to one restaurant and the other wants to go to a different restaurant.
- Both students are arguing over whose fault it is that a picture got torn.

Activity 3. *Conflict Resolution Advertisements:* Direct students to break up into groups of 3-4. Have each group choose a particular conflict resolution strategy such as compromise, brainstorming, agreeing to disagree, mediation, getting help from an adult, etc. and create an "advertisement" for it on a poster board. Hang these around the room.

Activity 4. *Conflict Resolution Storytelling:* Have students sit in a circle. Explain that the group will be participating in a mutual story-telling exercise regarding a conflict and its resolution. One person will begin a story with two (2) sentences. The person sitting next to her/him will add two (2) more sentences to the story and the story-telling will continue around and around the circle describing the conflicting situation. When the facilitator says, "Time to resolve!" students will continue the story two (2) sentences at a time but this time they will describe how the conflict gets resolved. Remind students to include an empathy component in the story.

Activity 5. *Letter of Apology:* Instruct students to think of a conflict that they have had with someone recently. Ask them to write a letter of apology including several statements about how that other person must have felt and what it was that other person might have been thinking or wanting. Letters do not have to be sent unless the student wishes to do so.

EMPATHY AND CONFLICT RESOLUTION

REPRODUCIBLE WORKSHEETS:

Worksheet 10.1, *Evaluating Conflict Resolution Styles*, directs students to identify the advantages and disadvantages of several conflict resolution styles. These include compromise, brainstorming, agreeing to disagree and getting help from a grown-up.

Worksheet 10.2, *Lots of Ways to Settle a Conflict*, asks students to draw four (4) pictures of solutions to a problem that two students are having.

Worksheet 10.3, *Win-Win*, asks students to read solutions to conflicting situations and to identify the "win-win" solutions and the "win-lose" solutions.

Worksheet 10.4, *Conflict Resolution Word Search*, invites students to find words related to conflict resolution in a word search.

Worksheet 10.5, *Ranking My Conflict Resolution Skills*, instructs students to cut out five (5) skills that are needed in resolving conflicts and glue them to a picture of a flagpole in the order which they perceive the level of their skill. The five (5) skills are listening to the other person's point of view, keeping myself calm, being willing to compromise, apologizing and thinking of lots of different solutions.

EVALUATING CONFLICT RESOLUTION STYLES

TYPE OF CONFLICT RESOLUTION	ADVANTAGES	DISADVANTAGES
Find some kind of middle ground so that both parties get some of what they want (compromise)		
Think of several other solutions to the problem other than the two ideas that the conflicting parties have (brainstorming)		
Decide that both parties have the right to their own opinions (agree to disagree)		
Ask an adult to settle the conflict (getting help)		

LOTS OF WAYS TO SETTLE A CONFLICT

DIRECTIONS: Two students are arguing over whose turn it is to look at a new book in the classroom. Draw four (4) solutions to this problem.

SOLUTION #1	SOLUTION #2

SOLUTION #3	SOLUTION #4

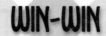

WIN-WIN

A "win-win" solution is one where both people are happy about the outcome. Both people feel as though they got what they wanted.

A "win-lose" solution is one where only one person likes the outcome and feels like s/he "won." The other person doesn't like the outcome and feels like s/he "lost." One person is happy and the other person is unhappy with the results.

DIRECTIONS: *Read the following situations and write WW in the spaces to the left of the solutions that describe "win-win" solutions and WL in the spaces to the left of the solutions that describe "win-lose" solutions.*

1. _____ John asks Tremica if he can play on her basketball team. Tremica explains that there would be too many people on her team to all be on the basketball court at the same time. John says that he really wants to play so she agrees to rotate the players so everyone can have a turn, including John.

2. _____ John asks Tremica if he can play on her basketball team. Tremica explains that there would be too many people on her team to all be on the basketball court at the same time. John says that he really wants to play but Tremica tells him he is a loser and to go away.

3. _____ Both Mark and Gilberto want the last cupcake. Mark says that he didn't get one but Gilberto says that he didn't have lunch and is really hungry. Mark grabs it and takes a big bite out of it.

4. _____ Both Mark and Gilberto want the last cupcake. Mark says that he didn't get one but Gilberto says that he didn't have lunch and is really hungry. They decide to cut the cupcake into two (2) pieces and share it.

5. _____ Anna and Jessica are working on a poster for a social studies project. Anna wants to color the background blue so that it will look like the sky but Jessica wants to color it red so that it will be bright. Jessica tells Anna that her idea is stupid and quickly picks up a red crayon and starts coloring.

6. _____ Anna and Jessica are working on a poster for a social studies project. Anna wants to color the background blue so that it will look like the sky but Jessica wants to color it red so that it will be bright. They talk about other colors that might look good and decide on purple.

CONFLICT RESOLUTION WORD SEARCH

DIRECTIONS: *Find these words related to conflict resolution in the word search.*

AGREE	LISTEN	COMPROMISE
EMPATHY	FEELINGS	MEDIATE
NEGOTIATE	RESOLUTION	SETTLE
WINWIN	UNDERSTAND	

```
N  P  U  E  L  W  X  C  I  A  E  Q  H  D  U  C
E  E  Z  U  H  F  P  E  C  D  D  N  F  S  N  O
T  I  T  D  O  N  E  G  O  T  I  A  T  E  D  M
N  W  W  M  H  U  R  H  A  M  H  V  W  T  E  O
I  Z  C  E  W  F  E  S  A  A  E  S  H  T  R  V
F  P  O  C  S  D  E  P  U  M  S  R  T  L  S  K
D  A  M  T  H  A  D  E  R  E  S  E  O  E  T  I
N  G  P  J  E  T  S  I  L  D  N  D  P  R  A  L
T  R  R  E  S  O  L  U  T  I  O  N  S  Y  N  S
F  E  O  Q  G  J  S  E  W  A  N  U  P  N  D  S
S  E  M  T  A  L  O  N  K  T  J  G  B  G  T  D
B  P  I  P  M  E  I  E  S  E  N  S  S  L  I  T
A  S  S  X  A  W  E  N  T  N  J  R  M  R  R  Y
N  W  E  E  L  T  R  E  S  N  K  A  S  W  P  Q
R  D  H  I  O  T  H  I  F  J  L  I  S  T  E  N
B  I  R  A  N  D  L  Y  M  G  S  Y  E  E  I  A
```

RANKING MY CONFLICT RESOLUTION SKILLS

DIRECTIONS: Cut out the various conflict resolution skills in the boxes below. Think about how well you do each one. Then glue them on to the picture of the flagpole with your best skill on the top, your second best skill right under it, your third best skill under the second one, finally gluing the skill that you need the most work on at the bottom.

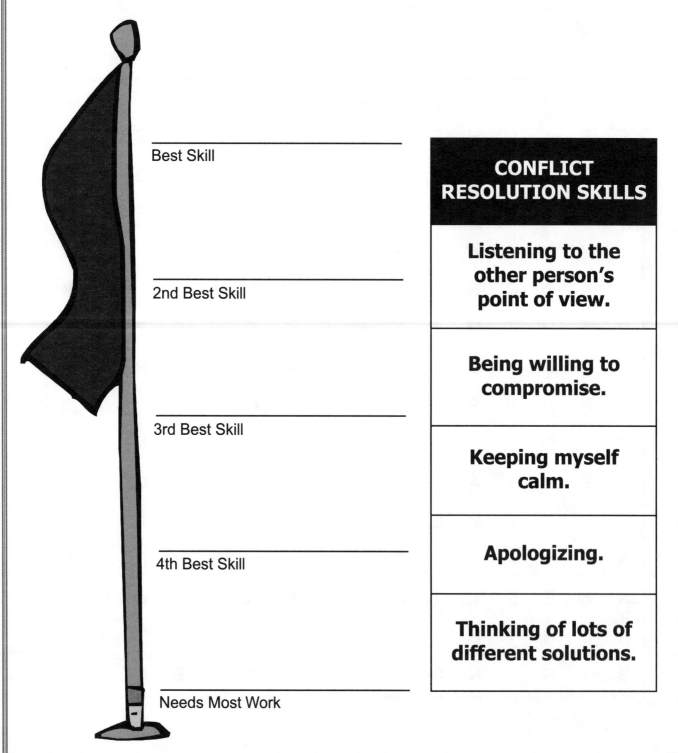

Best Skill

2nd Best Skill

3rd Best Skill

4th Best Skill

Needs Most Work

CONFLICT RESOLUTION SKILLS
Listening to the other person's point of view.
Being willing to compromise.
Keeping myself calm.
Apologizing.
Thinking of lots of different solutions.

EMPATHY AND ACCEPTING DIVERSITY

OBJECTIVES:

At the end of this lesson students will be able to:

- Identify that many of the same "groups" have differences and many members of the different "groups" have similarities
- Describe the many different "shapes and sizes" of people
- Be sensitive to inequalities among groups
- Verbalize the perspective of another person who is different from themselves

RATIONALE:

Increasing globalization makes it essential that students learn to be culturally sensitive and to understand the view points of other cultures. In addition, the passage of the American Disabilities Act makes it important for students to become comfortable working with others with disabilities. It is never too early to begin discussions of prejudice, discrimination or, more simply, the things that make people different. Empathy is essential for reducing prejudicial behaviors. Research suggests that empathy for diverse populations is enhanced if students are made aware of similarities between themselves and those children from other ethnicities and if they value and have positive opinions of those groups (Batson, Lishner & Cook, 2005; Hahn, 1980; Staub, 1986; Sturmer, Snyder & Kropp, 2005). It is critical that students learn that a race or a handicap is not the whole person.

MATERIALS:

Copies of Bingo cards in Appendix G, pencils, a child's story regarding immigration (i.e. First Crossings by Pam Munoz Ryan), journals, different colors of construction paper, scissors and magazine/newspaper pictures of different kinds of people.

SCRIPT:

People come in all shapes, sizes and colors. That is what we call diversity. Some of the ways that people are different are in the areas of race, religion, language, culture, lifestyle, neighborhood, family, talent and disability. Sometimes when we don't understand one of these differences we say that we don't like it or them. But we can learn so much from one another! And, even though we are all different, there are many ways that we are alike.

DISCUSSION QUESTIONS:

- Have you ever had a friend who was a different gender from you? Who was in a different grade from you? In what ways were you alike?
- Have you ever had a friend who had a different religion from you? What was it? What did you learn from that friend?
- Have you ever had a friend who was in a wheelchair or had some kind of handicap? What fun things did you do with that person?
- Do friends have to be exactly the same? Why or why not?

EMPATHY AND ACCEPTING DIVERSITY

ACTIVITIES:

Activity 1. *A Wacky Story of Prejudice :* Read and discuss the following story:

Once upon a time there was a smart and handsome blonde boy named Andrew whose family had just moved to a town called Brownsville. The third morning that they were in their new town Andrew woke up excited to start his first day at Coco Elementary School. His mother drove him to school and, as they went inside, Andrew noticed that many of the students avoided eye contact and seemed to frown at him. When he was being enrolled, he noticed that the secretary looked at his hair and shook her head. When he reached for last year's school yearbook to look at, the secretary shouted, "Don't touch that!"

As he entered the classroom for the first time, his teacher, Ms. Brown, told Andrew to sit in the back of the room with all the other blondes. Andrew didn't understand because he had always made good grades in the past, but he did as he was told. All morning Ms. Brown helped the dark haired students and ignored the blonde students. Once Andrew tried to raise his hand to ask a question but the teacher snapped at him and told him to put his hand down and do his work.

At recess all of the dark haired children grabbed the swings and the balls. Andrew noticed that the blonde haired children simply walked around with nothing to do. Once he tried to join in a soccer game but one of the dark haired boys said, "Get out of here! We don't let wimpy-looking blondes play! Go back where you came from!" Finally Andrew walked over to a sad-looking blonde haired boy and introduced himself. When Andrew asked him why he wasn't playing, the boy replied, "If you're blonde you're not allowed to play with any of the good stuff so I just don't play anything at all. I hate being blonde. When I grow up I want to dye my hair brown and move to another city."

At the end of the day Andrew stood in the back as kids lined up to go outside to be picked up by their parents. When his mom pulled up, he flopped himself in the seat and started to cry. He heard his mother say, "Andrew, wake up. Wake up. You're having a bad dream." Andrew opened his eyes and saw that he was in his old room and had never moved to Brownsville. He gave his mom a hug and breathed a big sigh of relief.

Discuss the story with the students. Ask them how they think Andrew felt and how they think the brown-haired children felt. Ask if this story is similar to anything really going on at their school.

Activity 2. *Differences and Similarities:* Ask students to stand together in a group. Explain that you will be asking certain people to step away from the main group in order to form another group. Each time that you ask a category of persons to form another group state, "Notice who is standing with you. Notice who is not. Notice how you feel." After you have completed the exercise, bring everyone back together and discuss. Here are a list of suggestions (but feel free to add your own!):

EMPATHY AND ACCEPTING DIVERSITY

a. "Step away from the group if you are a female."
b. "Step away from the group if you have ever been seriously ill."
c. "Step away from the group if you have ever been called fat."
d. "Step away from the group if one of your parents has ever served in the military."
e. "Step away from the group if you were raised Catholic."
f. "Step away from the group if you are Jewish."
g. "Step away from the group if one of your parents has ever been out of work for any reason."
h. "Step away from the group if you are Native American."
i. "Step away from the group if you are African American."

Activity 3. *Diversity Bingo:* Make copies of the DIVERSITY BINGO cards in Appendix G. Give each student one card. Have students walk around the room asking other students if they fit any of the categories on the Bingo cards. If they do, have the student holding the card mark off that square(s) with the student's name. The first person to get four in a row calls out "Bingo!" Discussion after the game can focus on how people can have multiple identities.

Activity 4. *Hear from an Expert:* Invite someone with a disability (i.e. someone in a wheelchair, someone with diabetes, someone with a birth defect, someone who is blind, someone who is hearing impaired, etc.) to speak to the students. Be sure to have a question and answer time.

Activity 5. *Understanding the Struggles of Immigration:* Read a children's book regarding immigration. Have students write a journal entry as if they were the immigrant in the story. Remind them to use feelings words in addition to thinking words. One recommended story is First Crossings by Pam Munoz Ryan.

Activity 6. *All Shapes and Sizes:* Prior to meeting with the students, have lots of pictures of people of various ethnicities, genders, sizes, abilities, etc. already cut out from magazines, newspapers, etc. and spread them over a large table. When meeting with the students, pass out five (5) different colors of construction paper to each student. Instruct them to draw and then cut out one geometric shape per color of paper – i.e. a circle, a square, a rectangle, a triangle, a hexagon, etc. Explain that it is okay to make these geometric shapes various sizes as well. When all of the geometric shapes are cut out, ask students to select a variety of five (5) of the already cut-out pictures of people and glue them onto their five (5) geometric shapes (one picture per geometric shape). Follow this activity with a discussion about how people come in all kinds of shapes, sizes and colors. If possible, create a bulletin board with everyone's shapes. Ask the group what they would like to title it.

Activity 7. *Multicultural Treasure Hunt:* Organize a multicultural treasure hunt around the school with information to be found in various locations.

EMPATHY AND ACCEPTING DIVERSITY

REPRODUCIBLE WORKSHEETS:

Worksheet 11.1, *Just Like Me,* directs students to identify other people who are like themselves in specific ways. Some of these likeness categories include hair color, height, favorite TV shows, academics, brothers & sisters, hobbies and problems.

Worksheet 11.2, *Put Yourself in Someone Else's Shoes,* asks students to think of someone who is very different from themselves and to draw themselves in that person's shoes. It then asks students to identify their feelings and to connect this experience with how they might treat the other person.

Worksheet 11.3, *Write a Telegram,* invites students to think of a less privileged person and to write a telegram to the President advocating for that person.

Worksheet 11.4, *Respecting and Blending Differences,* uses the metaphors of a salad and an orchestra to highlight the point that diversity creates good things. Students are asked to draw pictures and answer questions regarding how the multiple number of ingredients makes both a salad and an orchestra even better.

Worksheet 11.5, *Where Have We Been?,* Instructs students to look at a North American map and mark the places that they have been and to ask others to do the same.

JUST LIKE ME

DIRECTIONS: *Sometimes it is easier to feel empathy towards others who are like us. But everyone is like us in one way or another! Name some people who are like you in the following ways:*

Has the same hair color as you _____

Is the same height as you _____

Watches the same TV shows as you _____

Is good at the same subject as you _____

Has the same number of brothers and sisters as you _____

Likes the same hobbies as you _____

Has had 2 of the same teachers as you _____

Goes to bed at the same time as you _____

Has had a similar problem as you _____

PUT YOURSELF IN SOMEONE ELSE'S SHOES

DIRECTIONS: *Think of someone in your school who is very different from you. Maybe the person you are thinking of is a different race or a different gender or has a disability. Now imagine yourself as that person. In fact, draw yourself as that person (putting yourself in their shoes):*

How does it feel to be this person? _____

How does putting yourself in that person's shoes change how you will treat her/him?

_____

_____

WRITE A TELEGRAM

DIRECTIONS: *Think of a person who is less privileged than you (someone of a different race, someone living in poverty, someone handicapped, someone with a serious illness, etc.). Now use the "telegram" below to write an important message to the President about this person's needs, urging him to change something in government to make this person's life easier.*

WESTERN UNION
TELEGRAM

To: The President

From: _____

I am writing on behalf of _____

I would like to request _____

_____

_____

_____

                                        Sincerely,

                                        _____

97

RESPECTING AND BLENDING DIFFERENCES

Draw a picture of some of the different ingredients that go in a salad.

What would a salad be like with only one (1) or two (2) ingredients?

_____

_____

How does having lots of ingredients make a salad better?

_____

_____

Draw a picture of some of the instruments that go in an orchestra.

What would an orchestra be like with only one (1) or two (2) instruments?

_____

_____

How does having lots of instruments make an orchestra better?

_____

_____

How does having lots of different kinds of people make a get-together better?

_____

_____

WHERE HAVE WE BEEN?

DIRECTIONS: *Using a colored pencil of your choice (only one color please!) or dot stickers, put dots on the places where you have lived. Then ask several classmates to also select a colored pencil and mark where they have lived. Make a key at the bottom of the page.*

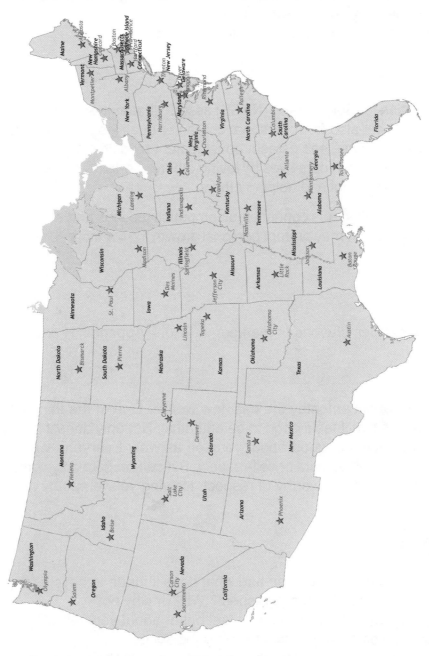

KEY

Color:_____	Person: _____
Color:_____	Person: _____
Color:_____	Person: _____
Color:_____	Person: _____

EMPATHY AND DEVELOPING SELF-RESPECT

OBJECTIVES:

At the end of this lesson students will be able to:

- Identify personal feelings associated with demonstrating empathic behaviors
- Identify ways that they are empathic people
- Clarify positive personal attributes and their growth

RATIONALE:

The National Association for Self-Esteem (NASE) asserts that authentic self-esteem comes not only from accomplishments, but also from personal character qualities such as empathy. NASE (2006) maintains that children increase self-esteem development by cultivating sensitivity and concern for others. Perhaps we learn to love ourselves by loving others. Certainly there is a certain kind of "high" that comes from being prosocial and helping others.

It is important that we help students connect their empathic feelings and behaviors with their feelings of self-respect. This realization may prompt personal growth from a more "I" orientation to a more "we" orientation.

MATERIALS:

Copies of Appendix F, paper, crayons or markers, scissors, Appendix H and dark colored paper

SCRIPT:

We have learned a lot about empathy the past few weeks. One of the things that I hope you have realized along the way is that it feels good to be empathic. Not only does it help you to feel closer to other people, it makes you feel good about yourself as well. Everyone wants to feel good about themselves. This is called self-esteem or self-respect. But self-respect only comes after you have felt, thought and done things that are worthy of respect. Helping your empathy grow will help you grow your self-respect!

DISCUSSION QUESTIONS:

- What does the word respect mean and what does it mean to have it for yourself?
- Do you think that bullies have self-respect? Why or why not?
- How does doing good things make you feel better about yourself? And how does feeling better about yourself make you want to do good things?
- Can you think of a time when you showed empathy and liked yourself more because you did? Can you think of a time when you didn't show empathy and liked yourself less because you didn't?

EMPATHY AND DEVELOPING SELF-RESPECT

ACTIVITIES:

Activity 1. *Connecting Positive Behavior to Character:* Have the students break up into pairs. Using the list of ideas in Appendix F ask one of the students to describe the details of a friendly behavior that s/he has done recently. Have her/his partner respond by saying, "Then you must be a really *<generous, thoughtful, kind, brave, friendly, etc.>* person" (whichever adjective is most appropriate). Then have the students reverse roles so that both students get to hear something positive about themselves as a person.

Activity 2. *Framing Me:* Ask students to draw pictures of themselves sticking up for someone (this can be a actual scenario or a made-up scenario). Then as a "frame" for the picture instruct students to write the feeling word that they would feel if they actually did this.

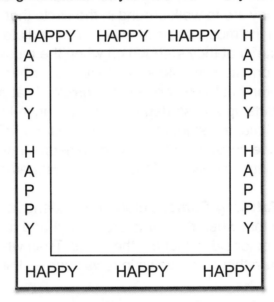

Activity 3. *What Others Like about Me:* Ask students to cut out a string of paper dolls holding hands. (This can be done by folding a piece of paper back and forth like a fan, but make sure that the sections of the paper between folds is wide enough to cut a shape of a person. Make sure that the "hands" touch the fold.) Have students write the name of a person that they care about on one side of each of the paperdolls. On the other side of each paperdoll have students write down what that person likes about them.

Activity 4. *Self-Respect Stepping Stones:* Prior to meeting with the students, cut out 8 – 10 shapes that resemble "stepping stones." Number the "stepping stones" so that each one has a different number. Then on the other side of each "stepping stone" write one (1) of the following questions/statements (or feel free to use your own questions/statements):

- What have you learned about empathy over the last several weeks?
- Which of the following feelings best describes how you feel about yourself now that you are using more empathy – happy, proud, strong, kind, friendly or caring?
- What would others say about your empathy now?

EMPATHY AND DEVELOPING SELF-RESPECT

- How can empathy make you feel better about yourself?
- Give yourself a pat on the back for learning more about empathy.
- What do you think is the most important part of empathy for you?
- How has empathy made you a better friend?
- Say out loud, "I have respect for myself because I know how to use empathy!"
- Say out loud, "I am proud of myself for being an empathic person!"
- Which of the three (3) parts of empathy – (1) "reading" others' feelings, (2) letting myself feel others' feelings and (3) saying or doing something supportive – do you think that you are the best at?

When meeting with students, place these "stepping stones" in a circle with the numbered side facing up. Ask students to find a "stepping stone" to stand on and explain to them that when the music plays they are to walk around in the circle that has been created by the "stepping stones." When the music stops they are to immediately stop walking and remain on the "stepping stone" that they stepped on when the music ceased to play. Ask the student who is standing on "stepping stone" #1 to turn over her/his "stepping stone" and to read the question/statement to someone in the group. That person responds to the question. Then the music starts up and students begin walking in the circle again. When the music stops the second time, the student on "stepping stone" #2 turns over his "stepping stone" and reads the question/statement to someone in the group who has not yet answered a question. Continue until all of the questions/statements have been used.

Activity 5. *Self-Respect Matching Game:* Before the students arrive, photocopy Appendix H onto dark colored paper (so that when the cards are cut out and turned over, the words will not be able to be seen from the other side). Cut out the cards. Then when the students are ready to play, mix up the cards and turn them face down in rows such as this:

Choose a fair way to decide who will go first in the game and then direct students to turn over two (2) cards when it is their turn. If a match is found, the student should tell a time when s/he exhibited that behavior and how s/he felt about her/himself when doing so. That student will then remove the matching cards from game. If a match is not found, the student must return the cards face-down to their original spot. Continue playing until all cards have been removed from game.

EMPATHY AND DEVELOPING SELF-RESPECT

REPRODUCIBLE WORKSHEETS:

Worksheet 12.1, *Benefits of Empathy,* instructs students to select words from a Word Box in order to complete sentences naming the benefits of empathy. Certain letters from those words are circled and students must then write down the circled letters in box at the bottom of the page. After writing all of the circled letters, the final benefit of empathy is revealed – "Empathy gives you self-esteem." This activity reviews the different features of empathy and its importance.

Worksheet 12.2, *Sticking Up for Someone,* invites students to think about what they might say in order to stick up for various individuals who are getting bullied. It then asks students how they would feel about themselves if they stuck up for someone.

Worksheet 12.3, *Who I Am and Will Be,* directs students to evaluate themselves on several continuums both how they perceive themselves now and how they would like to see themselves in the future. The continuums include selfish-generous, cruel-caring, trouble-maker-helper, talker-listener, distant-close, cold-hearted-warm-hearted, taker-giver, hyper-calm, indifferent-understanding.

Worksheet 12.4, *My Empathy Growth,* asks students to evaluate their skills in reading others' feelings, feeling others' feelings and saying/doing supportive things both before their lessons on empathy and since their lessons on empathy. This is done by coloring levels measured by a ruler and allows students to see their growth.

Worksheet 12.5, *Empathy Flipper,* uses origami to create the classic children's "flipper."

Directions: (a) Cut out the large square, (b) Turn the square face down and fold each of the four (4) corners to the middle so that they all touch (you should only see colors and numbers), (c) Turn flipper over and fold the four (4) corners to the middle again (you should only see numbers), (d) Fold this small square in half with the numbers in the middle; open and fold in half the other way again with the numbers in the middle. Students should now be able to slip their fingers under the colors in order to manipulate it.

Working in pairs students ask their partner to choose a color. Spelling the color, the student opens and closes the flipper in the two (2) different directions with each letter. As the last letter of the color is spelled the student opens the flipper and asks the partner now to choose one of the visible numbers. After the partner has chosen a number the student opens and closes the flipper in the two (2) different directions as s/he counts up to the number that the partner has selected. At the last count, the student opens the flipper and asks the partner to choose another visible number. At this point the student lifts the flap of the number that the partner has selected and asks whether s/he would like the number's top or bottom portion. When the partner has selected top or bottom, the student reads the question and the other person answers it. Partners should take turns manipulating the flipper and answering questions.

BENEFITS OF EMPATHY

DIRECTIONS: Use the words from the Word Box below to complete the sentences. Then write the circled letters in the spaces at the bottom of the page. It spells out a very important benefit of having empathy!

WORD BOX		
EMPATHY	READ	FEEL
SAY	OTHERS	FRIEND

1. Empathy helps me to ___○___ ___ other people's facial expressions and gestures in order to know their feelings.

2. Empathy helps me to○___ ___ things to others that are supportive.

3. Empathy helps me to care about ___○___ ___ ___ ___.

4. Empathy helps me to ___○___ ___ others' feelings along with them.

5. Empathy helps me to be a better ___ ___ ___○___ ___.

6. ___○___ ___ ___ ___ ___ helps me to better understand others.

Write down the letters that are circled.

EMPATHY GIVES ME SELF-___ ___ ___ ___ ___ ___.
     1   2   3   4   5   6

STICKING UP FOR SOMEONE

Bullying is a terrible thing but many kids do get bullied. Part of the reason that this happens is because other kids are afraid to speak up. One way to show empathy and feel good about yourself is to stick up for others.

DIRECTIONS: *In the bullying situations described below, write down what you could say in order to stick up for the person.*

(1) Maria and her family came from Mexico and she doesn't speak English very well. Some kids are teasing her about the funny way she talks. What could you say to stick up for her?

(2) Karl is in a learning disabilities class and is learning many interesting things but kids make fun of him and call him "Stupid." What could you say to stick up for him?

How do you feel about yourself when you stick up for someone? _____

_____

WHO I AM AND WILL BE

DIRECTIONS: *Each end of the horizontal lines below represents two extreme ends of a personal quality or trait. Most of us fall along the line somewhere in the middle – we are not at either end. Using a blue crayon or marker, place an 'X' on the lines where you feel you are today. Then with a red crayon or marker, place another 'X' on the lines where you would like to be as a grown-up. Be honest!*

Selfish --- **Generous**

Cruel --- **Caring**

Trouble-Maker --- **Helper**

Talker --- **Listener**

Distant --- **Close**

Cold-Hearted -- **Warm-Hearted**

Taker --- **Giver**

Hyper -- **Calm**

Indifferent --- **Understanding**

MY EMPATHY GROWTH

DIRECTIONS: *Think about how your empathy used to be before you started working on it. Then think about how it is now in the areas of reading others' feelings, feeling others' feelings and saying/doing something supportive. Using the ruler below color the lines measuring your before and after levels of empathy. See how much you have grown!*

Before	Now	Before	Now	Before	Now
READING OTHERS' FEELINGS		**FEELING OTHERS' FEELINGS**		**SAYING OR DOING SOMETHING SUPPORTIVE**	

EMPATHY FLIPPER

DIRECTIONS: *(a) Cut out the large square, (b) Turn the square face down and fold each of the four (4) corners to the middle so that they all touch (you should only see colors and numbers), (c) Turn flipper over and fold the four (4) corners to the middle again (you should only see numbers), (d) Fold this small square in half with the numbers in the middle; open and fold in half the other way again with the numbers in the middle. Students should now be able to slip their fingers under the colors in order to manipulate it.*

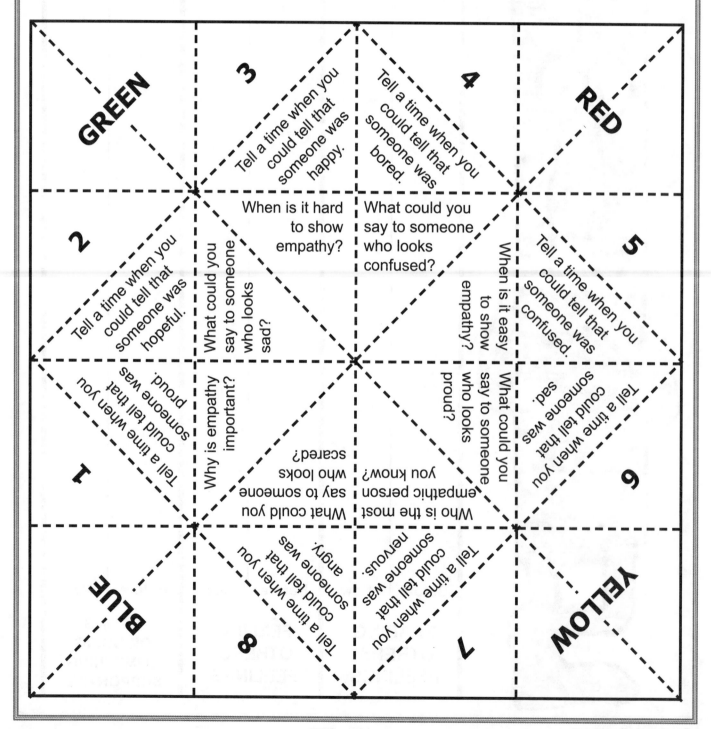

REFERENCES

REFERENCES

Attili, G. (1990). Successful and disconfirmed children in the peer group: Indices of social competence within an evolutionary perspective. *Human Development References, 33,* 238-249.

Bandura, A., Caprara, G.V., Barbaranelli, C., Gerbino, M. & Pastorelli, C. (2003) Role of Affective Self-Regulatory Efficacy in Diverse Spheres of Psychosocial Functioning. *Child Development, 74*(3). 769-782.

Batson, C.D., Lishner, D.A. & Cook, J. (2005). Similarity and Nurturance: Two possible sources of empathy for strangers. *Basic and Applied Social Psychology, 27*(1), 15-25.

Black, H. & Phillips, S. (1982). An intervention program for the development of empathy in student teachers. *The Journal of Psychology, 112,* 159-168.

Denham, S.A. (1998). *Emotional Development in Young Children.* New York: Guilford Press.

Denham, S.A. & Burger, C. (1991). Observational validation of teacher rating scales. *Child Study Journal, 21,* 185-202.

Eisenberg, N., Fabes, R.A., Carlo, G. (1993). The relations of empathy-related emotions and maternal practices to children's comforting behavior. *Journal of Experimental Child Psychology, 55*(2), 131-150.

Eisenberg, N., McCreath, H. & Ahn, R. (1988). Vicarious emotional responsiveness and prosocial behavior: Their interrelations in young children. *Personality and Social Psychology Bulletin, 14,* 298-311.

Fabes, R.; Eisenberg, N.; & Miller, P. (1990). Maternal correlates of children's vicarious emotional responsiveness. *Developmental Psychology, 26,* 639-648.

Farver, J.M. & Branstetter, W.H. (1994). Preschoolers' prosocial responses to their peers' distress. *Developmental Psychology, 30,* 334-341.

Feshbach, N.D. (1997). Empathy, the formative years: Implications for clinical practice. In A.C. Bohart & L.S. Greenberg (eds.), *Empathy Reconsidered: New Directions in Psychotherapy* (pp. 33-59). Washington DC: American Psychological Association.

Griffin-Shirley, N. & Nes, S.L. (2005). Self-esteem and empathy in sighted and visually impaired preadolescents. *Journal of Visual Impairment & Blindness, 99*(5), 276-285.

Hahn, S. L. (1980). Let's Try a Positive Approach. *Foreign Language Annuals, 13*(5), 415-417.

Hartup, W.W. & Laursen, B. (1992). Contextual constraints and children's friendship relations. ERIC Document number ED 310 848.

REFERENCES

Kaukianen, A., Bjorkqvist, K., Lagerspetz, K., Osterman, K., Salmivalli, C., Rotherberg, S., & Ahibom, A. (1999). The relationship between social intelligence, empathy, and three types of aggression. *Aggressive Behavior 25*: 81-89.

Klimes-Dougan & Kitner, 1990. Physically abused preschoolers' responses to peers distress. *Developmental Psychology, 26*, 599-602.

Kohn, A. (1991) Caring Kids: The Role of the Schools. *Phi Delta Kappan 72*(7), 496-506.

Kremer, J.F. & Dietzen, L.L. Two approaches to teaching accurate empathy to undergraduates: teacher-intensive and self-directed. *Journal of College Student Development 32*, 69- 75.

Leith, K.P. & Baumeister, R.F. (1998). Empathy, shame, guilt, and narratives of interpersonal conflicts: Guilt-prone people are better at perspective-taking. *Journal of Personality, 66*(1), 1-37.

Liff, S.B. (2003). Social and Emotional Applications for Developmental Education. *Journal of Developmental Education, 26*, 28-34.

Litvak-Miller, W. & McDougall, D. (1997). The structure of empathy during middle childhood and its relationship to prosocial behavior. *Genetic, Social & General Psychology Monographs, 123*(3), 303-324.

Main & George, 1985. Responses of abused and disadvantaged toddlers to distress in agemates: A study in the daycare setting. *Developmental Psychology, 21*. 407-412.

National Association for Self-Esteem (NASE). 2006 Retrieved April 13, 2006. http://www.self-esteem-nase.org/mag01.shtml

Paleari, F.G., Regalia, C. & Fincham, F., (2005). Marital Quality, Forgiveness, Empathy, and Rumination: A Longitudinal Analysis. *Personality and Social Psychology Bulletin, 31*(3), 368-378.

Pecukonis, E.V. (1990). A cognitive/affective empathy training program as a function of ego development in aggressive adolescent females. *Adolescence, 25*(97), 59-74.

Portner, J. (1997). Violence-prevention program reduces aggressive behavior, study concludes. *Education Week, 16*(36), 7.

Rogers, C.R. (1951). *Client-centered therapy*. Boston:Houghton-Mifflin.

Sagi, A. & Hoffman, M.L. (1976). Empathic distress in newborns. *Developmental Psychology, 12*, 175-176.

REFERENCES

Salmon, S. (2003). Teaching empathy: The PEACE Curriculum. *Reclaiming Children and Youth, 12*(3), 167-173.

Schutte, N.S., Malouff, J.M., Bobik, C., Coston, T.D., Greeson, C., Jedlicka, C. & Rhodes, E., Wendorf, G. (2001). Emotional intelligence and interpersonal relations. *Journal of Social Psychology, 141*(4), 523-536.

Staub, E. (1986). A conception of the determinants and development of altruism and aggression:Motives, the self, the environment. In C. Zahn-Waxler (Ed.) Altruism and aggression: *Social and biological origins.* Cambridge, MA: Cambridge University Press.

Staub, E. (1995). The roots of prosocial and antisocial behavior in persons and groups: Environmental influence, personality, culture, and socialization. In W. Kurtines & J. Gewirtz (Eds.), *Moral Development.* Boston: Allyn and Bacon.

Strayer, J. & Roberts, W. (1989). Children's empathy and role-taking: Child and parental factors and relations to prosocial behavior. *Journal of Applied Developmental Psychology, 10,* 227-239.

Stürmer, S., Snyder, M., & Kropp, A. (2005). Empathy-motivated helping: The moderating role of group membership. *Personality and Social Psychology Bulletin, 32*(7), 943-956.

Vreeke, G.J. & van der Mark, I.L. (2003). Empathy, an integrative model. *New Ideas in Psychology, 21,* 177-207.

Wied, M., Goudena, P.P. & Matthys, W. (2005). Empathy in boys with disruptive behavior disorders. *Journal of Child Psychology & Psychiatry & Allied Disciplines, 46*(8), 867-880.

Zahn-Waxler, C. & Radke-Yarrow, M. (1982). The development of altruism: Alternative research strategies. In N. Eisenber (Ed.), The development of prosocial behavior (pp. 109-137). New York: Academic Press.

Zahn-Waxler, C. & Radke-Yarrow, M. (1990). The origins of empathic concern. *Motivation and Emotion, 14,* 107-130.

APPENDIX

PARENT LETTER

Dear Parent;

Your child has been participating in an Empathy Development program. In order for children to learn a new skill and make it "stick" it is helpful for them to hear about it and practice it in more than one setting. Reinforcing at home what your child has learned through this program will help your child "internalize" the information – and consequently become more empathic. Some suggestions for you to consider are:

✓ Be responsive to your child's needs. This is empathy in action!

✓ If your child's misbehavior affects another person, ask how s/he thinks the behavior made the other person feel.

✓ Help you child develop a large vocabulary of feelings words. Exaggerate your own use of feelings words.

✓ Read children's books to your child that incorporates messages of kindness, brotherhood/sisterhood, and connection to others (a suggested reading list is included)

✓ Encourage your child to "read" others' feelings. You can practice this by looking at pictures in books and magazines and playing a game where you take turns telling how you think the person feels.

✓ If your child has hurt another child, ask your child to consider how her behavior has hurt the other. Instead of focusing on the misbehavior per se, focus on the other person's feelings.

✓ Point out similarities between your child and other children. (Research shows that empathy increases when one perceives the other as similar to the self.)

✓ As a family, practice doing Random Acts of Kindness for others. Talk about how good it feels to do nice things for others.

✓ Encourage your child to show an interest in others' activities and feelings.

✓ If your child tells you of another child who is ill or having some sort of difficult circumstance, take a few moments and help your child make some sort of Get Well/Sympathy/Encouragement card for the other child.

Sincerely,

PARENT LETTER
CONTINUED...

RECOMMENDED CHILDREN'S READING FOR EMPATHY DEVELOPMENT

Cazet, D., A Fish in His Pocket
Published by Scholastic Inc. www.scholastic.com

Christiansen, C., The Mitten Tree
Published by Fulcrum Publishing www.fulcrum-books.com

DeBell, S. How Do I Stand in Your Shoes
Published by Youthlight, Inc. www.youthlightbooks.com

DiSalvo-Ryan, D., Uncle Willie and the Soup Kitchen
Published by Harper Collins Children's Book Group www.harpercollinschildren.com

Havill, D., Jamaica's Blue Marker.
Published by Moughton Mifflin Company http://houghtonmifflinbooks.com

Hughes, S., Alfie and the Birthday Surprise.
Published by Harper Collins Children's Book Group www.harpercollinschildren.com

Joosse, B. M., Better With Two.
Published by Harper Collins Children's Book Group www.harpercollinschildren.com

Keats, E.T., Louie.
Published by Penguin Group Inc. http://us.penguingroup.com

Munsch, R., Zoom
Published by Scholastic Inc. www.scholastic.com

Munsch, R., Ribbon Rescue
Published by Scholastic Inc. www.scholastic.com

Pfister, M., Rainbow Fish
Published by North-South Books, Inc. www.northsouth.com

Stroud, B., Down Home at Miss Dessa's
Published by Lee & Low Books, Inc www.leeandlow.com

Zolotow, C., I Know a Lady
Published by Harper Collins Children's Book Group www.harpercollinschildren.com

FEELING WORDS

HAPPY

delighted	joyful	festive	jolly	playful
contented	satisfied	enthusiastic	inspired	glad
comfortable	pleased	happy	cheerful	excited

ANGRY

irritated	annoyed	furious	enraged	angry
sulky	aggravated	upset	bothered	mad
exasperated	displeased	indignant	bugged	put out

SCARED

fearful	alarmed	scared	frightened	timid
nervous	anxious	worried	chicken	afraid
horrified	petrified	uneasy	terrified	tense

SAD

depressed	discouraged	gloomy	moping	low
downcast	low-spirited	unhappy	moody	sad
dejected	downhearted	blue	miserable	

INTERESTED

engrossed	interested	attracted	fascinated	nosy
involved	intrigued	absorbed	captivated	curious

HELPLESS

helpless	inferior	incapable	defenseless	useless
powerless	vulnerable	forced	exposed	weak

STRONG

strong	empowered	capable	assertive	certain
resilient	solid	competent	able	tough

NONSENSE PHRASES

(1) Ouhay rewirt carol you

(2) wherup shaldoit catastro bucket

(3) zapi doudaw plumaria sharing

(4) jumpy didey harpest

(5) carlie that bilbow up

(6) therawop to you siggy

(7) can whole gabber teel

(8) cheesey hope candle do it

(9) offer not peril vit

(10) shaping cat bottle up

(11) adept didly tootsie dada

(12) boat garby quarter huff

GREEK CHORUS

NARRATOR: Jack and Jill went up the hill to fetch a pail of water.

CHORUS: They felt excited.

NARRATOR: Jack fell down.

CHORUS: Jack felt embarrassed; Jill felt worried.

NARRATOR: And broke his crown.

CHORUS: They felt scared.

NARRATOR: And Jill came tumbling after.

CHORUS: Jill felt fearful.

NARRATOR: Up got Jack and home did trot.

CHORUS: Jack felt hopeful.

NARRATOR: As fast as he could caper.

CHORUS: Jack felt anxious.

NARRATOR: He went to bed and bound his head

CHORUS: Jack felt tired.

NARRATOR: With vinegar and brown paper.

CHORUS: Jack felt silly.

TRASH

SUPPORTIVE

SUPPORTIVE

"I want to go first!"	"Would you like to go first?"
"You don't need to cry about it!"	"Are you OK?"
"You probably cheated."	"Congratulations!"
"Whatever."	"I'm happy for you."
"So what?"	"I'm sorry that happened to you."
"You should see what I did!"	"You did a great job on that."
"The new kid looks like a geek."	"Let's go introduce ourselves to the new kid!"
"You shouldn't put it there!"	"I'm sorry."
"Just forget about it."	"Can I help you find it?"

SUPPORTIVE

"Are you crazy?"	"It's an interesting idea."
"My idea was better."	"What a great idea!"
"Who cares?"	"That's too bad."
"You have to do it my way."	"Let's see if we can use both of our ideas."
"You really stink at this."	"Keep trying!"
"You must not be very smart."	"I used to have a lot of trouble with that too."
"Can't you do that?"	"I have a hard time with that too."
"Don't be such a crybaby."	"Is there anything I can do?"
"You've got to be kidding!"	"I'm glad that you brought him."

FRIENDLY BEHAVIORS

Helping

Letting others go first

Letting others choose what to play

Complimenting

Sharing

Inviting others to join you at recess

Inviting others to your house

Listening

Sticking up for others

Introducing yourself & others

Smiling

Waving or saying, "Hi"

Including others who get left out

Encouraging

Telling the truth

Handling disagreements agreeably

Apologizing

Keeping secrets

Calling on the phone

Waiting for others

BINGO CARD #1

Oldest in the family	Has been to another country	Speaks another language besides English	Has someone of a mixed racial heritage in their family
Knows someone of a different religion than their own	Has been to a wedding ceremony	Has been to a funeral	Likes food from another country
Has very dark hair	Likes movies WITHOUT violence	Has taken care of a sick person	Knows someone who has been treated for a drug or alcohol problem
Knows someone who is homeless	Plays a musical instrument	Has more than 5 pets	Has been treated in the hospital's emergency room

BINGO CARD #2

Likes gymnastics	Has been to another country	Plays a musical instrument	Has been to a wedding ceremony
Knows someone of a different religion than their own	Oldest in the family	Knows someone who has been treated for a drug or alcohol problem	Likes food from another country
Speaks another language besides English	Likes movies WITHOUT violence	Has taken care of a sick person	Has held the door open for someone else
Knows someone who is homeless	Has been treated in the hospital's emergency room	Has allergies	Has dark skin

BINGO CARD #3

Likes gymnastics	Has been to another country	Plays a musical instrument	Speaks another language besides English
Has held the door open for someone else	Youngest in the family	Knows someone who has been treated for a drug or alcohol problem	Has been treated in the hospital's emergency room
Has dark skin	Knows someone of a different religion than their own	Has taken care of a sick person	Has parents who are divorced
Knows someone who gets free lunch at school	Walks home from school	Is an only child	Likes food from another country

BINGO CARD #4

Walks home from school	Has been to another country	Knows someone who gets free lunch at school	Speaks another language besides English
Has held the door open for someone else	Likes food from another country	Knows someone who has been treated for a drug or alcohol problem	Is an only child
Has dark skin	Has been teased or bullied	Has a parent that has been in the military	Has parents who are divorced
Has taken care of a sick person	Has played with someone in a wheelchair	Has been to a wedding ceremony	Has been to a funeral

BINGO CARD #5

Doesn't get to see one of his / her parents very often	Knows someone who is homeless	Knows someone who gets free lunch at school	Doesn't like video games
Has played with someone in a wheelchair	Likes food from another country	Speaks another language besides English	Has been to another country
Has been to a funeral	Has a friend of the opposite sex	Has a parent that has been in the military	Has held the door open for someone else
Likes to dance	Has someone of a mixed racial heritage in their family	Has been teased or bullied	Has allergies

BINGO CARD #6

Is interested in other religions	Knows someone who is homeless	Knows someone who gets free lunch at school	Doesn't get to see one of his / her parents very often
Doesn't like video games	Likes food from another country	Likes to dance	Has been to another country
Has a friend of the opposite sex	Has taken care of a sick person	Has a parent that has been in the military	Has been teased or bullied
Has an unusual pet (not a cat, dog or fish)	Has someone of a mixed racial heritage in their family	Has played with someone in a wheelchair	Has allergies

FRIENDLY BEHAVIORS MATCHING GAME

SHARE	**SHARE**
COMPLIMENT	**COMPLIMENT**
HELP	**HELP**
STICK UP FOR SOMEONE	**STICK UP FOR SOMEONE**
INVITE	**INVITE**
LET FRIEND GO 1ST	**LET FRIEND GO 1ST**

FRIENDLY BEHAVIORS MATCHING GAME

APOLOGIZE	**APOLOGIZE**
HUG OR PAT	**HUG OR PAT**
LISTEN FOR FEELINGS	**LISTEN FOR FEELINGS**
HOLD THE DOOR FOR SOMEONE	**HOLD THE DOOR FOR SOMEONE**
WAIT	**WAIT**
GAVE A GIFT	**GAVE A GIFT**